DATE DUE

			PRINTED IN U.S.A.

GIFTS COOKS *love*

GIFTS COOKS

love

Recipes for Giving

Sur La Table with Diane Morgan

Photography by Sara Remington

Andrews McMeel
Publishing, LLC
Kansas City · Sydney · London

For Doralece, whose heart and soul
guided the creation of this book.

10 11 12 13 14 SDB 10 9 8 7 6 5 4 3 2 1

ISBN: 978-0-7407-9350-9

Library of Congress Control Number: 2010924493

Design: Ren-Whei Harn and Diane Marsh
Photography: Sara Remington
Photo Assistant: Stacy Ventura
Art Director: Jennifer Barry
Food Stylist: Kim Kissling
Assistant Food Stylist: Tina Stamos
Prop Stylist: Kerrie Sherrell Walsh
Assistant Prop Stylist: Lori Engels

Gifts Cooks Love, *Tips Cooks Love*, *Things Cooks Love*, and *Baking Kids Love* are all trademarks
belonging to Sur La Table, Inc. of Seattle.

www.andrewsmcmeel.com
www.surlatable.com

ATTENTION: SCHOOLS AND BUSINESSES
Andrews McMeel books are available at quantity discounts with bulk purchase for educational, business,
or sales promotional use. For information, please write to: Special Sales Department, Andrews McMeel
Publishing, LLC, 1130 Walnut Street, Kansas City, Missouri 64106.

CONTENTS

INTRODUCTION

Just think of all the occasions we have for giving a gift—bridal shower, wedding, birthday, housewarming, Christmas or Hanukkah, Mother's Day, Father's Day, Valentine's Day, anniversary, bar or bat mitzvah, get-well-soon, new baby, graduation, retirement, hostess gift, thank-you gift—and no reason at all. Tangible expressions of caring and love can be wrapped and given in so many ways. In the best of all worlds, the gift connects the recipient and giver, joyfully communicating a personal bond. At a minimum, it acknowledges an occasion or obligation. Regardless, a handmade gift, especially a food gift, represents creative energy and time spent in the kitchen—a homemade hug.

Giving food gifts can be as simple as knocking on your neighbors' door with a gift of just-canned peach jam and thanking them for collecting your mail while you were away on vacation, and as ritualized as an annual tradition of baking a huge batch of highly anticipated Christmas pecans for friends, family, and colleagues. It's the personal connection of sharing a homemade gift and wrapping it up in some special way that brings joy and delivers goodness and cheer.

An added bonus to all this creativity and kitchen wizardry is that homemade food gifts are affordable—a very cost-effective way to acknowledge and celebrate an occasion. Even a modest investment of time, which is all that many of the food gifts in *Gifts Cooks Love* require, and a growing movement toward buying seasonally, at farmers' markets and through CSAs, means a cost savings on ingredients.

For instance, the savvy cook knows that the bargain-priced, end-of-season green tomatoes in the market are terrific when preserved and turned into Green Tomato Chutney (page 53). In the same way, a neighbor's walnut or crabapple tree, laden with green walnuts or an overabundance of fruit, is the beginning of a barter-style, gift-giving exchange. The green walnuts provide the basis for exotic Italian Nocino Liqueur (page 143), while the crabapples are transformed into a cinnamon-spiced accompaniment to a holiday ham.

Camaraderie is another benefit of making food gifts. There are even some folks who have preserving parties. Gathering a fun group, begin a weekend morning at a U-pick farm, and then join together to process and preserve the fruit or vegetables and turn out a counter full of luscious fruit jams or savory sauces. The laborious chore of peeling and pitting fruit becomes a gabfest rather than tedious solo time in the kitchen. Many hands make light work, and many hands produce a greater volume of finished preserved foods. The gift exchange begins!

Gifts Cooks Love is for the cooking novice as well as the experienced cook. For the novice, an entire chapter is devoted to No-Cook Gifts (though kitchen skills are helpful for the Homemade Garganelli on page 156). And easy, tempting liquid sensations are provided in the Drink Gifts chapter starting on page 133. Someone with a taste for liqueurs, who is long on patience but short on cooking skills, is the perfect candidate for making Limoncello (page 135) or Italian

Nocino Liqueur (page 143). With a gallon-size glass jar and a brief list of ingredients, you are on your way to bringing some jolly good holiday cheer. And it only takes measuring spoons and cups to delight your friends with spice blends, such as the Bollywood Coconut Curry Popcorn Seasoning on page 151, the Moroccan Spice Blend on page 153, or the Backyard BBQ Rub on page 155. Even the Seven-Month Vanilla Extract on page 159 is the perfect, simple-to-make gift. If you can nudge some plump vanilla beans into a flask-style bottle and fill it with vodka, you are almost done making a delightful and incredibly useful gift for friends who like to bake.

For the bakers and candy makers, *Gifts Cooks Love* is filled with gift projects you may never have thought to make at home. Consider graham crackers. Those classic childhood favorites are good enough from the box, but truly astonishing when homemade. As cute as could be, the Cinnamon-Coated Graham Crackers on page 113 are dotted with tiny holes, fluted at the edges, and cracker-y crisp. Fluffy and fun Homemade Toasted Coconut Marshmallows (page 121) are pillowy treats compared to the standard store-bought ones. And caramel-dipped apples can't even compete when tasted against the Roasted White Chocolate–Dipped Apples on page 127. They aren't a trick; they're a real treat for any Halloween party host.

For the DIY person who loves to smoke and cure, indulge your family and friends (and, of course, yourself) with the fun cooking projects in Chapter 7. Pull out your stovetop smoker to make bottles of Smoky Tomato Ketchup (page 71), or rub and cure your own bacon starting with a pork belly from your local butcher shop. For those with access to fresh fish, you'll have Olive Oil and Herb–Cured Albacore Tuna (page 79). Wild-caught salmon becomes brunch-worthy Salmon Gravlax (page 77) with a little salt, sugar, gin, and curing time.

At the end of the book, you'll find a chapter of ideas for gift giving called Make-a-Gift Kits. Expanding on all the tempting food gifts included in the book, combine these luscious foods creatively, as well as discover packaging ideas and imaginative ways to bundle and present gifts. It's easy to wrap a jar with ribbon and tie a bow, but if that jar were Arrabbiata Sauce (page 63) nestled in a colander with a package of artisan dried pasta and a hunk of Parmesan cheese, how much more fun and gift-worthy that would be. Creative gift giving starts in the kitchen, is packaged with a flourish, and is delivered with exuberance and fun.

From our kitchen to yours, our gift to you is a book full of family- and friend-tested recipes, broken down into manageable steps, delivered with tips, notes, and packaging details. We hope that you derive pleasure from creating these gifts, finding your time in the kitchen to be playful and fun and sharing your efforts with those you love and care for. After all, giving a food gift comes from the heart.

CHAPTER 1

THE *gift*-GIVING KITCHEN

THE GIFT-GIVING KITCHEN

This chapter introduces you to the tools and equipment we used to make the recipes in this book. Carefully review the annotated list to see what you already have and what you'll need to add to your existing inventory.

Bench Scraper

We use a bench scraper, a handy kitchen tool used when baking and making pasta, to divide dough, scrape and clean the work surface when working with pastry and cookie dough, and loosen stuck dough. A quality bench scraper has a wide, comfortable handle made of either nonslip rubber or wood, a stainless-steel blade, and, ideally, inch increments on the blade for measuring.

Brownie Pop Molds

To make the Double Fudge Brownie Pops on page 89, you'll need to buy the silicone molds made by Wilton. For gift giving, it makes sense to buy two or three molds since each mold makes just eight brownie pops. These molds could also be used for baking other sweet treats, creating ice pops, ice-cream bars, or gelatin shapes.

Canning Jar Lifter

These specialized tongs are used to safely raise or lower jars into the boiling water bath. It is essential to have a sturdy, well-built jar lifter that won't slip. We prefer the ones with silicone handles.

Cheesecloth

Finely woven cloth made of 100 percent cotton has a number of uses in the gift-giving kitchen. It is used to make spice pouches, is helpful when straining liquids, and is wrapped around the Home-Churned Lemon-Herb Butter (page 149) while it rests.

Disposable Gloves

Use disposable surgical gloves or food-prep gloves when handling hot chile peppers to prevent the caustic compound (capsaicin) that is naturally present in chiles from irritating your skin. Wear them when working with dark-colored produce such as beets, cherries, and berries to keep your hands from being stained red. Look for surgical gloves at a pharmacy or either type of gloves in a large supermarket.

Fluted Pastry Cutter

Though not a critical tool, it certainly makes the fluted edges on the Homemade Garganelli (page 156) and the Cinnamon-Coated Graham Crackers (page 113) look adorable and homespun. This stainless-steel tool (with a 2½-inch wheel and comfortable-grip handle) easily cuts through dough, making a fluted, stylized cut that is perfect for pasta, pastries, cookies, and crackers.

Food Dehydrator

A food dehydrator is a fast, easy, and economical way to preserve the season's bounty. Slices of food are arranged on vented, stacking trays that allow the air to circulate. The best dehydrators have a fan that circulates the heated air throughout the dryer and across all food surfaces. Look for a model with an adjustable thermostat so that food can dry at the correct temperature and, ideally, with a 500-watt motor so food dries in hours, not days like some models.

Food Processor/Mini Food Processor

A food processor is a time-saver all the time, but especially during the holidays, when you may want to make a pâté, cheese dip, pastry dough, or the like. Unless you use it to make bread dough, you don't need a giant machine. The standard 11-cup model will meet nearly all preparation needs. A mini food processor is handy for chopping ginger and garlic and for pulverizing herbs with sugar, as is called for in the Boysenberry and Lemon Verbena Jam on page 43.

Funnels

You'll need both narrow-neck and wide-mouth funnels to complete the projects in this book. A narrow-neck funnel is essential for bottling the Seven-Month Vanilla Extract (page 159), the Smoky Tomato Ketchup (page 71), and the two liqueurs in the Drink Gifts chapter beginning on page 133. A wide-mouth funnel is used for canning, making the process of ladling hot preserves into sterilized jars clean and efficient.

Kitchen Scale

Measuring by weight is the most accurate method. The best kitchen scale is digital, and has both metric (grams) and U.S. (pounds and ounces) measurements, along with a tare feature. This feature allows you to weigh a bowl, zero out that weight, and then add an ingredient, giving you the net weight of that ingredient. It isn't critical to have a scale with a bowl attached; without an attached bowl you have the option of using different bowls or none at all. A scale is particularly useful in baking, for measuring chocolate, and for meats, such as the pork belly used for Benny's Bacon on page 73.

Kitchen Twine

Be sure to buy the proper kitchen twine—it should be 100 percent linen because linen resists charring and is sturdy. Flimsy string won't do, and dental floss isn't applicable to any kitchen preparation! You'll be surprised how often you will reach for twine once it is in the kitchen. We use it for cheesecloth pouches filled with spices, which can be tied to the side of a pot for easy removal. It's the right twine to use for trussing poultry and tying roasts.

Mandoline

This manual slicing tool is used to cut food into uniform thick or thin slices. Professionals use a large, stainless-steel, commercial-style mandoline, but for the home cook a simpler model is really all that is needed. A Japanese model made by Benriner is economical and versatile because it comes with three different cutting blades, adjusts for thick or thin slices, and, most important, includes a finger guard.

Onion Goggles

Many cooks cry buckets of tears when chopping onions and shallots. No more! Onion goggles may seem ridiculous until you try them. They are amazing—these dorky-looking, sturdy plastic goggles have a comfortable foam seal that protects the eyes from onion vapors. They have antifogging lenses for maximum clarity. The only drawback is that they won't fit over eyeglasses.

Parchment Paper and Nonstick Baking Liners

We recommend using nonstick baking sheets or lining a baking sheet with either parchment paper or a nonstick baking liner—Silpat is the best-known brand—to create an excellent nonstick surface. Parchment paper is less expensive, but with care, the good-quality nonstick baking liners will last for years.

Pasta Machine

Maybe we're old-fashioned, but we love the hand-crank, chrome-plated, Italian pasta machine that lasts for years and years. It efficiently rolls out beautiful sheets of pasta dough. The exact same machine is still sold, and it comes with an adjustable table clamp and attachments for cutting two widths of pasta—fettuccine and tagliatelle. Additional attachments are sold separately for cutting other shapes and sizes of pasta. There is even an electric attachment available for motorizing the machine.

Pastry Bag and Decorating Tips

If you like to decorate your baked goods for the holidays, buying a reusable waxed canvas pastry bag makes sense. You can also buy disposable pastry bags. Buy either individual decorating tips for hors d'oeuvres or desserts, or buy a set of tips to have for a lifetime. Ateco brand pastry tips are a popular brand with pastry chefs, and it's the brand we use in the kitchen.

Pressure Canner

It is essential to use a pressure canner when canning low-acid foods such as vegetables, meat, poultry, seafood, and the fabulous recipe on page 79 for Olive Oil and Herb–Cured Albacore Tuna. Greater heat exposure is required in order to destroy harmful toxin-producing bacterial spores. A pressure canner is a tall, thick-walled pot with a lid that locks in place and a pressure-regulating device. Pressure canners hold a minimum of four 1-quart canning jars and are also available in larger sizes holding up to seven 1-quart jars in one layer or eighteen 1-pint jars in two layers. There are two types of pressure canners: a weighted-gauge pressure canner and a dial-gauge one. For the recipes in this book, use a dial-gauge style with a visual gauge that indicates the pressure level.

Rimmed Baking Sheets

We couldn't live without the heavy, nonstick, aluminum rimmed baking sheets made by Chicago Metallic's Commercial line. They are workhorses in the kitchen for baking cookies, pastries, crackers, and the like. We suggest buying rimmed baking sheets as opposed to classic cookie sheets because they offer the most versatility. Use a silicone heat-proof spatula to lift baked items, so that you don't scratch the surface of the pan.

Rolling Pin

For pie and tart makers, high-quality tools make baking a pleasure. Invest in a heavy, thick pin made of hardwood or marble and at least 12 inches long. It's a tool for a lifetime. American-style rolling pins have handles, while French-style pins do not. Both work equally well; the type you choose is a matter of personal preference.

Slow Cooker

For those who love to make soups, stews, and braised dishes, an electric countertop slow cooker is an ideal appliance. It cooks food at a very low temperature over a period of several hours, and, best of all, once the timer is set and the power button is pushed it requires virtually no attention from the cook. Look for a model that has a timer that turns off the cooker when the cooking time is up and keeps the food warm until serving time. Slow cookers come in several sizes and at every price point. The 6½-quart size is ideal if you are cooking for a family or like to cook and freeze extra portions.

Spice or Coffee Grinder

Ideally, a cook has one small, electric coffee grinder dedicated to grinding spices and another one strictly used for grinding coffee beans. It's a bit of a luxury to have two, but you don't want the oils and particulate matter from grinding coffee to interfere with the delicate spice flavors that come from grinding whole spices. That said, the best way to clean your grinder is to add a few spoonfuls of uncooked rice to the grinder and pulverize it. Tap out the ground rice and the container and blades are clean.

Springform Pan

This pan is great for Panforte (page 103) and other cakes that are difficult to unmold, such as cheesecakes. Springform pans come in aluminum, stainless steel, or nonstick. We prefer the aluminum ones. For this book, you will need two 8-inch pans with 2-inch sides.

Stand Mixer

Look for a good-quality stand mixer. The best are sturdy, heavy, and dependable and come with three attachments—a whip, dough hook, and paddle. All three are used in this book. Consider buying an extra mixing bowl and an extra whip attachment so that you can swap out a used bowl or beater without needing to stop and wash the dirty one. This is especially helpful if you are making a cake that requires the yolks and whites to be beaten separately. A good mixer should be a lifetime investment. That said, you can get by with a handheld mixer for some of the recipes in the book.

Stovetop Smoker

This large, rectangular-shaped stainless-steel pan with a tight-fitting lid and sturdy handles that fold for easy storage includes a drip pan and wire rack. Used on top of the stove, with pulverized smoking chips, this smoker allows you to easily smoke fish, meats, poultry, and vegetables. We prefer the Camerons brand stovetop smoker and use the smoking chips that come with it. Buy Camerons's larger containers of chips when you need refills.

Strainers

It's great to have three sizes of strainers, all doing double duty for cooking and baking needs; having two that are fine-mesh is ideal. Use a large-mesh strainer for straining stocks with bones, and have a medium fine-mesh strainer for straining liquids or sauces from which you are trying to remove sediment and seeds. Use the small fine-mesh one for straining the liquid from soaked fruits and spices, such as mustard seeds, and it is great for dusting the tops of baked goods such as the Biscotti Christmas Tree (page 105).

Thermometers

Certain kitchen tasks require specific tools, and that is definitely the case when it comes to thermometers. Depending on the food gifts you decide to make, the right thermometer will be critical to success. These tools are inexpensive and amazingly useful—truly confidence builders for any cook because they take the guesswork out judging the degree of doneness.

Candy Thermometer: With a long stem and a clip that attaches to the side of a pot, this thermometer gauges the temperature of sugar syrups and candy mixtures. This is a critical tool for candy making because it measures the stages of a cooking sugar solution, and it also takes the guesswork out of custard making.

Instant-Read Thermometer: The small-dial, thin-shaft instant-read thermometer is the most accurate way to judge the doneness of meats, poultry, fish, egg custards, and the temperature of chocolate for tempering. You must not leave the thermometer in the food, however. Instead, you insert it, give it a few seconds to register the temperature, and then out it comes. For safety and sanitation, always wash the thermometer before reinserting it in any food. Many chefs prefer an analog thermometer to a digital one.

Oven Thermometer: If you doubt the accuracy of your oven's thermostat, buy an oven thermometer before you start cooking and baking. Once you know how far off the thermostat is, you can adjust the temperature dial accordingly. Whether your oven is brand-new or old, it doesn't hurt to have an oven thermometer to double-check its accuracy.

Water Bath Canner

While you can use any large, heavy pot with a lid and any wire rack that fits inside as a boiling water bath canner, the best bet for the cook who is interested in canning is to buy a genuine water bath canner. It's an excellent investment and, with proper care, will last for years. These large, deep pots are usually made of speckled enamel-coated metal or stainless steel. They come equipped with a basket-shaped rack that is designed to keep canning jars securely in place. The basket has folding handles that allow the rack to be elevated and hooked to the rim of the pot. The jars can be lowered into the water for canning and then lifted and kept elevated for easy removal. Look for a complete preserving kit if you are just getting started canning at home; the set comes with a steel boiler and canning jar rack, plus a canning funnel and jar lifter.

CHAPTER 2

THE *gift*-GIVING PANTRY

THE GIFT-GIVING PANTRY

Having the right ingredients in your pantry is an essential part of making a winning recipe. To get you started on your food gifts–making journey, here is an annotated list of the special ingredients used in this book.

151-Proof or 190-Proof Alcohol

Neutral grain spirits, such as Everclear, are a type of colorless, odorless alcohol distilled from cereal grains. They are sold, depending on state liquor laws, as either 151 proof (75 percent alcohol) or 190 proof, which is 95 percent alcohol and the highest alcohol content available. These are the perfect base for making infused spirits such as the Limoncello on page 135 and the Italian Nocino Liqueur on page 143. Both of these liqueurs are diluted after they are infused to reduce the alcohol content.

Albacore Tuna

The Pacific Northwest is known for its delicious, sustainably caught albacore tuna, which is shipped across the country and available from many fishmongers in the summer and early fall. It can also be shipped fresh directly to your door from Web sites like seafoodinc.com. This species of tuna is commonly canned and referred to as "white meat tuna." In my recipe for Olive Oil and Herb–Cured Albacore Tuna on page 79, you'll see that home-canned tuna is much moister and more flavorful, with a pale flesh that flakes easily for salads and pasta dishes.

Candied Orange Peel

Many specialty baking stores and gourmet shops carry candied orange peel. Thin strips of orange peel are boiled in water to remove the bitter flavor, cooked in sugar syrup to sweeten, and then rolled in sugar and left to dry. These crystallized orange candies are delicious dipped in chocolate or added to baked goods like the Panforte on page 103.

Citric Acid

Citric acid is a natural preservative found in many foods, especially lemons and limes. It is used in the powder form to help preserve canned foods that are low in acid, like the Arrabbiata Sauce on page 63. Look for the Fruit-Fresh brand, which is what was used in the recipes.

Crabapples

An exceptionally tart, firm fruit, crabapples look like miniature orchard apples. They come from crabapple trees that are cherished for landscaping purposes because of their small size and beautiful pink flowers. Since crabapples are high in pectin, they are usually made into jelly, but we find the acidic flavor ideal for pickling, as in the Cinnamon-Spiced Crabapples on page 46.

Crystallized Ginger

Also called candied ginger, crystallized ginger is available at specialty food stores and some well-stocked supermarkets. This method of sweetening and preserving ginger is done by simmering fresh ginger slices in sugar water, rolling the slices in coarse sugar, and then drying them. Crystallized ginger adds sweetness, a bit of spice, and crunch to desserts and baked goods, including the Mini Apricot and Crystallized Ginger Quick Breads on page 95.

Flax Seed

Though they are more commonly used to make linseed oil, whole flax seeds have a nutty flavor and add a delightful, healthy crunch to foods like Coconut Granola Crunch on page 100. Look for flax seed or ground flax seeds, rich in nutrients and omega-3 fatty acids, in the refrigerator case in health food stores or in large supermarkets with a natural foods section.

Gelatin

Gelatin is a clear, odorless protein rendered from the skin and bones of animals. It is most often found in powdered form, and it needs to be soaked in water and then heated to dissolve the granules before it's added to thicken desserts like Italian panna cotta or the Toasted Coconut Marshmallows on page 121.

Graham Flour

The three components of the wheat kernel—germ, bran, and endosperm—are ground separately, creating the coarse texture and distinct taste of graham flour. Named after Reverend Sylvester Graham, an early advocate of healthy eating in the 1830s, graham flour is richer in protein and nutrients than bleached white flour and coarser in texture than whole wheat flour, though the latter is often used as a substitute. For the Cinnamon-Coated Graham Crackers on page 113, we highly recommend seeking out graham flour, which is found at most health-focused food stores.

Green Tomatoes

Green tomatoes can refer to two types: the sweet, tender heirloom varieties such as Green Zebra, or the firm ones that would turn red if fully ripened. For the Green Tomato Chutney recipe on page 53, we're referring to the underripe variety. Those immature fruits that sadly hang from the vine at the end of summer are not to be missed and left to rot. Green tomatoes have a faint tomato flavor and dense, almost crisp, texture that is delicious fried or stewed.

Green Walnuts

Between May and the end of June, walnut trees are in bloom with lime-like green spheres that will eventually mature into hard brown walnut shells. It is at this stage—when the spongy interior has not yet produced a nut—that Italians traditionally pick green walnuts and immerse them in spiced alcohol to create *nocino*. To make the Italian Nocino Liqueur on page 143, we picked walnuts from our neighborhood trees; however, if you cannot locate a tree in your area, know that you can conveniently buy green walnuts online from Web sites such as localharvest.org.

Large-Flake Unsweetened Coconut

Look for wide-cut flakes of unsweetened coconut for the Coconut Granola Crunch on page 100 at natural food stores. It is quite different in texture and taste from sweetened shredded coconut and is perfect for this granola.

Liquid Pectin

Pectin is a natural gelling agent found in fruits and vegetables, especially citrus and apples. It is used to thicken and stabilize prepared foods like jam, jelly, marmalade, and candy. Though it is available in a powdered form, that version cannot be substituted for the liquid pectin used in the recipe for Blackberry-Merlot Jellies on page 119. Liquid pectin is available at most well-stocked supermarkets. We use Ball Brand or Sure-Jell Certo liquid fruit pectin.

Meyer Lemons

Originating in China, Meyer lemons have become increasingly popular in American cooking in the past few decades, thanks to the birth of "California Cuisine." Most commercially grown Meyer lemons available in the U.S. are grown in California, though they are grown in Texas and Florida as well. They are smaller, rounder, and a deeper shade of yellow-orange than regular lemons, plus their taste is less acidic and more fragrant. Look for them in late fall, winter, and early spring at most grocery stores.

Pimentón de la Vera Dulce

This sweet smoked paprika from southern Spain is dried for weeks over an oak fire and then ground to a fine powder. The resulting deep, rich flavor is a little sweet, a little spicy, and a little smoky. It is delicious in almost any savory dish, but it adds a special depth of flavor and intensity to the Moroccan Spice Blend on page 153.

Porcini Mushrooms

The prized, distinctly woody, nutty flavor and acerbic aroma of porcini mushrooms make them popular in Italian dishes like risotto and pasta. Drying porcinis preserves their shelf life so that they can be enjoyed outside of the season when they are foraged in the wild. At the market, look for thick, firm white stems and broad brown caps that are meaty and have a pungent, sour aroma. See page 83 for the Dried Porcini Mushrooms recipe.

Pork Belly

The fat-laced meat from the belly of pigs is cured to make American bacon. Though you may find it at specialty butcher shops, you will probably need to special order the whole belly, which weighs around 10 pounds, to prepare Benny's Bacon on page 73.

Pulverized Wood Smoking Chips

For use in a stovetop smoker, be sure to purchase the small, pulverized wood chips rather than larger chunks. Brands like Camerons include chips with the purchase of a smoker, and refills can be purchased at cookware stores or ordered online.

Saffron

It takes about 14,000 hand-picked stigmas of the crocus flower to produce 1 ounce of saffron, the most expensive spice in the world. Luckily, each dried thread goes a long way in Mediterranean dishes like paella, bouillabaisse, and tagines, contributing an intoxicating flavor and vibrant golden hue. A little is used in the Moroccan Spice Blend on page 153.

Salts

It is helpful to keep several types of salt stocked in your kitchen. Within easy reach of the stove or prep counter keep kosher salt or fine sea salt for all your cooking tasks. For baking, table salt or fine-grained sea salt works best. At the table, it is lovely to have a finishing salt such as *fleur de sel* for sprinkling on foods. Curing salt need not be a kitchen staple as it is used specifically in this book for curing bacon.

Curing Salt: Different brands of curing salt contain unique formulas, but in essence it is a combination of salt and either sodium nitrite or sodium nitrate that is used to preserve meats. The nitrite or nitrate inhibits bacterial growth and helps preserve the color of cured meats. Curing salt is often dyed pink to differentiate it from ordinary table salt, since it can be harmful if consumed in large quantities.

Kosher Salt: An additive-free coarse salt, kosher salt is used by some Jews in the preparation of meat; in addition, for many gourmet cooks, this salt is preferred for its taste and texture. If measured and used in baking, by volume, one needs to use more kosher salt than table salt to achieve the same desired level of saltiness.

Sea Salt: Sea salt is in fact salt recovered through the natural evaporation of seawaters. It comes in either fine-grained or large crystals. By volume, use fine-grained sea salt interchangeably with table salt. Fleur de sel, from Brittany or the Camargue region of France, is one of the most prized sea salts, with large, flaky, grayish crystals and a pure, briny flavor and aroma.

Table Salt: The most common salt, table salt is a fine-grained, refined salt processed with additives to keep it from caking. (It may or may not have iodine added.) Many gourmet cooks prefer to use additive-free salt, either kosher or sea salt, because when tasted side by side, the purity of kosher or sea salt is quite obvious. However, there is no discernable difference in taste when used in baking.

Salmon

Whether a whole fish or a fillet, fresh salmon is labeled, according to United States Department of Agriculture (USDA) regulations, as either "wild" or "farmed." Beyond that, you might see little white signs stuck in the ice or on the package indicating the fish's origin, upbringing, and whether or not it is organic. Wild salmon will be Pacific salmon from California, Oregon, Washington, British Columbia, or, most likely, Alaska. (Or it might be caught by a sport fisherman with a license to fish for the few wild Atlantic salmon left in the rivers that feed into the Atlantic Ocean.) Farmed Atlantic salmon might be labeled organic if it is actually farmed salmon originating from the North Atlantic, off the coasts of Ireland, Nova Scotia, and Scotland. Although the USDA does not currently have organic seafood regulations in place, Europe has had organic certifying agencies since 1998. Salmon farms with organic certification must operate in adherence to a strict set of standards. Our preference is always to buy wild salmon because of the discernable textural difference in the fish: Wild salmon has a more muscular flesh than farmed salmon, which tends to be soft and a bit flabby.

Farmed salmon is available year-round while wild salmon is seasonal, with the peak between mid-May and mid-September. However, many Pacific fishermen and processors freeze their salmon within 45 minutes of catching it and are therefore able to keep fish markets supplied with wild salmon all year. Look for moist, glistening skin on fillets, and if the salmon is whole, look for eyes protruding bright and clear. It should smell fresh, not fishy. Don't be afraid to ask to sniff the fish before purchasing it.

Tipo "00" Flour

Farina di grano tenero tipo 00, literally, "flour of soft grain, type 00," under the Caputo brand, is one of only a few Italian 00 flours certified for use in making true Neapolitan pizza by the Association of Real Neapolitan Pizza, a group with 2,500 members worldwide. Caputo flour is 100 percent hard wheat with no enrichment. The protein, at 11.5 percent, is lower than most hard-wheat flours. This flour creates soft, delicate dough, very different from other dough recipes. Even using American all-purpose flour with an 11.7 percent protein level did not produce the same results, which is why this flour is recommended in the recipes for Rustic Rosemary-Parmesan Crackers on page 111 and Homemade Garganelli on page 156. Caputo flour is available at specialty food stores importing Italian foods and also online at www.fornobravo.com.

CHAPTER 3

DECORATIVE
packaging

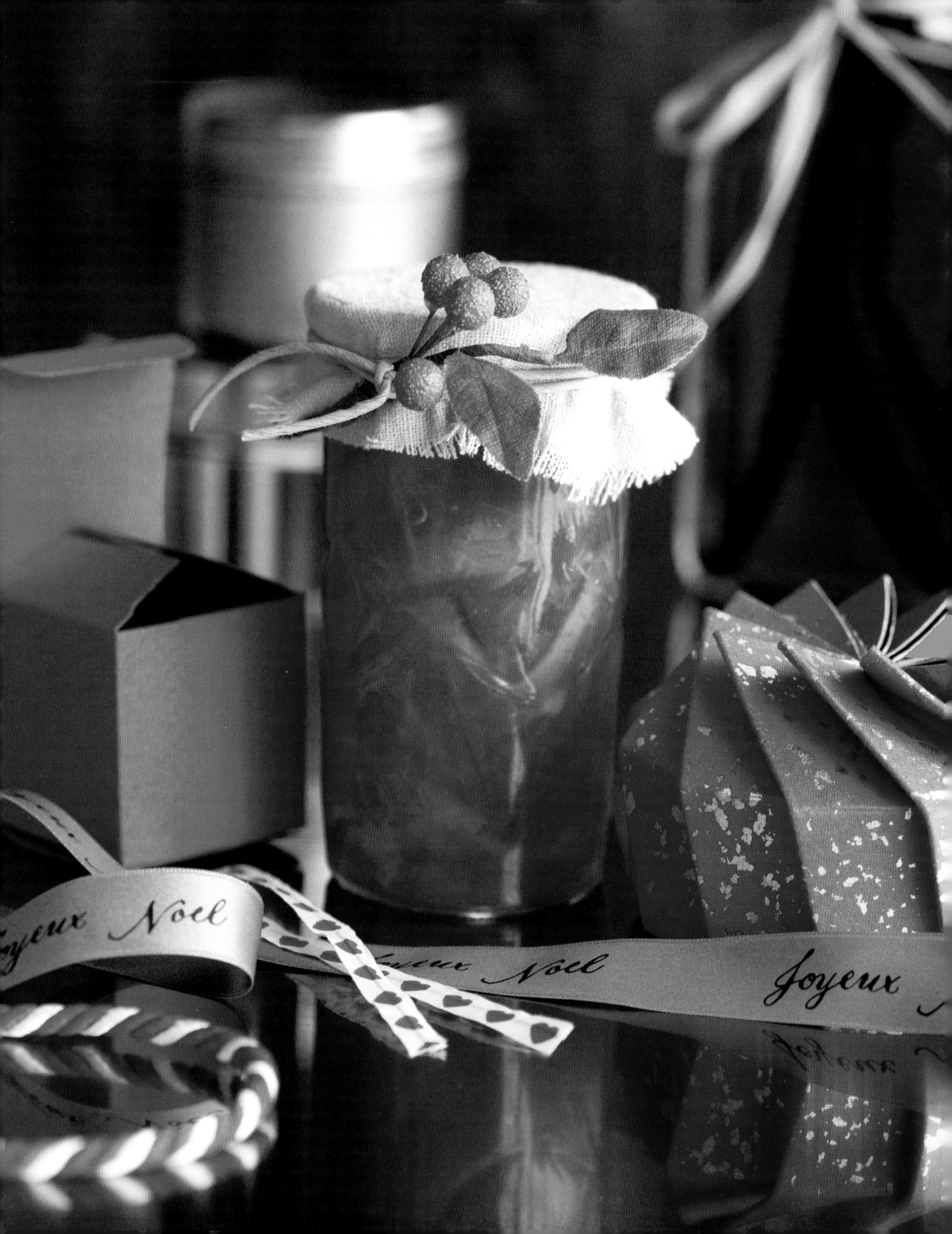
Noel
Noel
Joyeux

DECORATIVE PACKAGING

IMPLEMENTS

Bottles

Jars

Tins and Boxes

Pans

Unique Containers

Bags

Wrapping

Sticks

Ties

Labels and Cards

Beyond the creative cooking process and fun in the kitchen, the art of giving food gifts involves imaginative packaging the final flourish. Fanciful or restrained, your gift and how it is wrapped expresses an act of caring. After all, homemade gifts from the kitchen are, first and foremost, gifts from the heart. Here's where you get to play and be artistic and resourceful. We're always in awe when we see simple, everyday items recycled into clever packaging. For instance, for a holiday luncheon and gift exchange, a friend saved up paper towel rolls, filled them with cellophane-wrapped homemade caramels, tucked in a gift card to a local coffee shop, wrapped the rolls in festive paper, and tied each end with red grosgrain ribbon. They were adorable, contemporary, and looked like the English party crackers given as party favors.

Packaging doesn't need to be expensive or elaborate; it just needs to be inspired and inventive. Consider this chapter as a resource for all your gift-giving needs. We've tried to think out of the box, so to speak, providing you with ideas for how to bottle, can, bag, wrap, tie, and label your food gifts.

Bottles

You'll need glass bottles for several of the food and drink gifts in the book. We found old-fashioned recycled green glass bottles with hinge caps that are perfect for the Smoky Tomato Ketchup on page 71. The creased neck of these bottles reminds us of the old-style glass Heinz 57 ketchup bottles, bringing some wistful nostalgia to the gift. For the Seven-Month Vanilla Extract on page 159 and the Italian Nocino Liqueur on page 143, a clear glass, apothecary-style bottle seemed fitting. Flat-sided, flask-style bottles with a clasp closure top are a perfect shape. Liqueurs, such as Limoncello (page 135), look best presented in a sleek, tall bottle, befitting the elegance of the gift. Look for smooth, cylindrically shaped bottles with an airtight seal.

Jars

The recipes for home-preserved jams, marmalades, chutneys, sauces, pickled foods, and spiced fruits require canning jars. American-made glass jars with rubber-rimmed lids and screw-top bands are the standard for home canning. However, for gift giving, consider the German-made marquise-shaped canning jars made by Leifheit. Not only do the jars optimize shelf space, but they are also more unusual and gift-worthy. Alternatively, Italian-made glass canning jars with a hinged metal clamp and airtight, replaceable rubber gasket also work well for preserving. These jars are made by Bormioli Rocco. The Cinnamon-Spiced Crabapples on page 46 look especially good packed in this style of jar.

Gifts, such as the Apricot-Bourbon Mustard on page 59 or the Bollywood Coconut Curry Popcorn Seasoning on page 151, need to be packaged in smaller quantities and look best in condiment-size containers and spice jars. There are so many attractive shapes and sizes available. For example, consider giving the popcorn seasoning in a jar with a shaker top. Though the mustard can be packed into a bulbous-shaped jar, it could also be given in a white porcelain French mustard pot with a wooden spoon attached.

Tins and Boxes

At Christmastime, stores sell tins and laminated boxes in all shapes and sizes as festive packaging for homemade sweet treats and baked goods. Often, you'll see rolls of decorative waxed paper for sale to coordinate. If you plan ahead, you can even have your monogram imprinted on boxes. Another idea is to buy tins in solid colors and pick up special art pens that allow you to write on metal. Consider buying white tins and writing in gold ink or red tins and writing in white ink. Clear

paint cans, from a crafts store or ordered online, look great wrapped in decorative paper and are perfect as a year-round gift packaging option. The Cinnamon-Coated Graham Crackers on page 113 could be packaged in a white paint can, wrapped in red-and-white checked paper, and tied with navy blue ribbon as a fun summertime gift for a backyard barbecue. Bring along marshmallows and chocolate bars and have s'mores for dessert. Finally, a budget-friendly way to package baked gifts is to buy laminated Chinese takeout boxes or the ones made from recycled paper.

Pans

Though you can bake and give the Mini Apricot and Crystallized Ginger Quick Breads on page 95 in metal or ceramic loaf pans and make a homemade baked gift more elaborate by including the pan, too, the economical choice is to buy Italian-made paper loaf pans. These attractive, grease-proof paper loaf pans allow you to bake gifts right in the package. They come in several sizes, including mini loaf pans and shallow round cake pans that could be used for the Panforte on page 103.

The Jalapeño and Cheddar Skillet Cornbread on page 97 can certainly be baked in a skillet and then removed and given wrapped in cellophane, but consider how fun it would be to give the cornbread right in the pan. Small cast-iron skillets are relatively inexpensive, less than ten dollars, and would be perfect as a hostess gift, holiday gift, or thank-you gift for a weekend at a friend's cabin.

Unique Containers

The Honey Butter (page 97) and Home-Churned Lemon-Herb Butter (page 149) can be rolled into a log and wrapped in waxed paper with raffia ties, or rolled in plastic wrap and wrapped with a layer of parchment paper for a homespun look. Alternatively, consider packing the fresh butters as the French do, in an earthenware crock. These ceramic crocks allow butter to be stored without refrigeration for up to 30 days. The base is filled with cold water, which keeps the butter fresh and spreadable. It's a practical and a fun presentation.

Rather than packaging the Cracked Pepper, Dried Cherry, and Chocolate Chunk Biscotti (page 91) in a cookie tin, laminated box, or cellophane bag, consider giving it in an Italian biscotti jar. The Coconut Granola Crunch (page 100) could be given in big cereal bowls and the Homemade Garganelli (page 156) presented in a colander wrapped up with a big sheet of clear cellophane and tied with a bow. Present the Salmon Gravlax (page 77) or Benny's Bacon (page 73) on a wooden bread board sealed with a plastic or cellophane wrap and tied with a bow.

Bags

Petite, small, or large cellophane bags, whether clear, candy striped, or imprinted with seasonal motifs, are ideal for packaging some of the baked gifts in Chapter 8 as well as the confections and chocolate gifts in Chapter 9. The petite cellophane bags, often used for candies, are the perfect size for the Double Fudge Brownie Pops on page 89. Cinched with a seasonal ribbon, these brownie pops are ready for gift giving or as party favors. Use the large bags for Cracked Pepper, Dried Cherry, and Chocolate Chunk Biscotti (page 91) and tie them with a bright seasonal ribbon. Or

for a homespun look, arrange a dozen or more Rustic Rosemary-Parmesan Crackers (page 111) in a clear bag and tie it with raffia. The Toasted Coconut Marshmallows (page 121) would be adorable stacked like toy building blocks in a clear bag tied with an oversized bow.

Wrapping

You'll first want to tightly wrap the Salmon Gravlax (page 77) and Benny's Bacon (page 73) in plastic wrap to keep it fresh, but to make it gift-worthy, double wrap it with an interesting outer paper. Something as humble as butcher paper, brown craft paper, or parchment paper tied with raffia or thin wood rope dyed in earthy tones gives these cured and smoked presents a home-crafted feel, and that is exactly what these gifts are all about.

Sticks

Heatproof lollipop sticks are needed for the Double Fudge Brownie Pops on page 89. Look for these sticks in the baking section of well-stocked cookware stores; Wilton makes a good version. You'll typically see the heatproof sticks in white, though colored ones, if available, would be cute for special holidays, such as orange sticks for Halloween. Wooden ice-pop sticks, needed for the Roasted White Chocolate–Dipped Apples on page 127, are available at crafts stores. Occasionally, you'll see them in the baking aisles of supermarkets.

Ties

Let your imagination run wild and have coordinating raffia, ribbon, and other ties such as butcher's twine or thin wood rope. Look in hardware stores, crafts stores, stationery shops, and fabric centers with a large selection of cloth ribbon and trimmings. It is less expensive to buy grosgrain ribbon sold by the yard than to purchase it prepackaged from a card store. Even big box stores will sell commercial-size rolls of ribbon at holiday time. We've bought wide, white ribbon with big red polka dots that can double as holiday ribbon and as fanciful ribbon for a hostess or birthday gift.

Labels and Cards

Using unexpected materials to make labels and gift cards is another way to decorate a food gift in a delightful, nontraditional, and crafty way. A little Elmer's glue or fabric glue can go a long way toward turning layers of household paper, such as cut-up brown grocery bags and corrugated cardboard, into clever cards. You could buy several sheets of handmade paper and foil sheets from an art supply store and, with only a few dollars spent, turn out terrific-looking gift cards. Use a hole punch and ribbon tie a to attach a homemade card to your food gift! Use rubber stamps and plain labels purchased at office supply stores to create decorative labels. Gel drawing pens work well for hand-painting borders. With children to help, it becomes a fun family project.

CHAPTER 4

ESSENTIAL *tips* & TECHNIQUES
FOR PRESERVING AND DEHYDRATING

Preserving foods for long-term storage in either a water bath canner or a pressure canner is not as difficult as you might think, but does require special equipment, specific procedures, and safety guidelines. This chapter provides all the detailed information you will need to make any of the recipes in the book requiring a water bath canner, pressure canner, or food dehydrator.

Water Bath Canning

Though recipes such as the Aleppo Pepper–Peach Chutney on page 37 or the Cinnamon-Spiced Crabapples on page 46 can be made and kept in the refrigerator for several weeks without spoiling, the reason to take the next step and preserve these foods through "heat processing" is to prolong their shelf life. Instead of foods taking up space in the refrigerator or freezer, properly preserved foods can be safely stored in your pantry for up to a year. Water bath canning is the safe method used to preserve high-acid foods with a pH (acidity) of 4.5 or lower. Fruits, jams, jellies, and marmalades are high-acid foods, as are other fruits and vegetables with the addition of an acidic ingredient such as lemon juice or vinegar.

Preserving Kit and Accessories

Though it is possible to set up a water bath canner with any large pot and a sturdy wire rack that fits the inside bottom of the pot, having a preserving kit—which includes a water bath canner, canning jar rack, funnel, and jar lifter (see Chapter 2)—makes the process easier and safer. Additional accessories include a ladle, timer, durable hot pads, and a long, nonmetallic object for removing air bubbles. There are nonmetallic spatulas and "bubble removers" on the market for this purpose, but a plastic or wooden chopstick or skewer works just as well. A magnetic lid lifter is another optional utensil that makes it easy to lift lids out of hot water, though silicone-coated tongs work well, too.

Canning Jars

Canning jars and other styles of jars are described in detail in Chapter 3; in addition, selecting the appropriate size jar for the recipe you plan to make is important to consider here, especially when it comes to giving preserved food as gifts. For instance, decorative half-pint canning jars are perfect for the Côtes du Rhône–Rhubarb Compote on page 65 because the compote is used as a condiment and a 1-cup portion would be ideal for 4 servings. The Arrabbiata Sauce on page 63 is meant to be served with pasta, so a 1-pint or 1-quart jar would make the most sense, depending on whether the gift is for a couple or a family. When choosing jars, consider the portion size and how many servings you want to give.

Canning Instructions

These step-by-step directions are based on using the classic, American-made glass jars with rubber-rimmed lids and screw-top bands, otherwise known as "mason jars." For other types of canning jars, see the manufacturer's instructions. The canning steps for all jars will be the same; however, the sealing procedures will be different for hinge-topped jars with rubber gaskets and for one-piece lids with a food-safe sealing compound.

Step 1: Fill and Boil Water in a Water Bath Canner

Fill the pot half full for 1-quart jars or two-thirds full for pint and half-pint jars. Insert the wire canning rack so that the handles rest over the sides of the pot, cover, and bring the water to a boil over high heat.

Step 2: Preparing and Sterilizing Jars, Lids, and Screw Bands

Wash the jars, including the lids and screw bands, in hot, soapy water. Alternatively, run the jars through the regular cycle of your dishwasher, washing the lids and screw bands by hand. Once the water in the canner comes to a boil, carefully arrange the jars on the metal rack and lower them into the water. Boil for 10 minutes to sterilize, and then lower the heat to a simmer and leave the jars in the water until needed. Meanwhile, place the lids in a saucepan and cover them with water. Heat the water to a simmer, but do not boil, and then remove the pan from the heat and cover until needed. This process sterilizes the lids and softens the sealing compound on the underside of the lid. The screw bands do not need to be sterilized; keeping them at room temperature allows for easy handling.

Step 3: Filling and Sealing the Jars

1 When the recipe is prepared and ready for canning, use a jar lifter to remove one jar at a time from the canner. Tilt the jar and pour all the hot water in the jar back into the canner. Set the jar on a protected surface, such as a wooden cutting board or towel-lined, sturdy rimmed baking sheet. (Placing a hot jar on a cold work surface can create thermal shock and potentially crack the glass jars.) To avoid contaminating the sterile jars, do not manually dry them or touch the inside of the jar.

2 Set a wide-mouth canning funnel in the jar and ladle in the food (in the case of canning tuna, the raw fish needs to be hand packed into the jars). It is important to leave the necessary headspace noted in each recipe to allow the food to expand and bubble during processing.

3 Run a wooden skewer or other long, non metallic object around the inside edges of the filled jar to release any air bubbles that may be trapped in thick or chunky foods. If necessary, add more food or liquid to the jar.

4 If needed, use a clean, damp paper towel to wipe the entire rim of the jar clean to ensure a proper seal. Use a magnetic tool or silicone tongs to remove a lid from the water and position it on the jar so that the sealing compound is centered on the rim.

5 Place a screw band on the jar and tighten just until fingertip-tight. Tightening the lids too firmly means the jars can't vent, which potentially leads to the seals' failing.

6 Repeat this process until all the jars are filled.

Step 4: Processing

Place the sealed jars on the canning rack and carefully lower the rack into the simmering water. The water must cover the jars by at least 1 inch, preferably 2 inches, throughout the processing time. Add more hot water if necessary. Cover the canner and increase the heat to bring the water back up to a boil. Once the water has reached a full rolling boil, process the jars for the time specified in the recipe. This will kill all microorganisms in high-acid foods and ensure that the jars are sterile. Turn the heat off at the end of the processing time and remove the canner lid, but leave the jars in the hot water for an additional 5 minutes so that they begin to cool and the pressure stabilizes. With durable hot pads, lift the rack with the jars onto the edge of the canner. Use a jar lifter to remove the jars from the rack without tilting them. Transfer the jars to a wooden cutting board or towel-lined rimmed baking sheet to cool. Don't wipe the jars dry at this point; most of the water will evaporate from the heat, plus you will risk breaking the seals. Let the jars cool in a draft-free place for about 24 hours.

Step 5: Checking the Seals

After the jars have cooled, check to be sure they have sealed. Remove the screw bands and press down on the center of each lid. If the lid is sealed, it will be concave and won't move from the pressure of your finger. You can also lift the jar by the lid to ensure that it is sealed. If it is secure, the seal won't break, regardless of the weight of the jar. If the seal is broken, then either refrigerate the jar and use it within a few days or reprocess it following the same instructions. Be advised, though, that the quality of reprocessed foods will diminish; we don't recommend giving reprocessed jars as gifts.

Step 6: Storing Preserved Foods

Remove the screw bands and wipe the jars clean. If needed, use a cloth dampened with vinegar to remove any tough stains or residue on the jars. Wipe the jars again with a clean, damp towel. Wash and dry the screw bands. It is not necessary to keep the screw bands on jars that will sit on a shelf undisturbed; however, for gift giving, we like to screw the bands back on. They not only give the jar a finished look but also protect the lid and seal during transport. Label the jars, noting the contents and the date it was preserved. Home-canned foods are best kept for up to 1 year in a cool, dark place.

Pressure Canning

Low-acid foods (pH 4.6 and higher) require pressurized heat to kill all bacteria, including botulism. Foods like vegetables, meat, poultry, and fish require this method. The Olive Oil and Herb–Cured Albacore Tuna on page 79 is the only recipe in this book that requires pressure canning. However, a pressure canner is a terrific and necessary piece of equipment for those who like to preserve vegetables, such as beets, peppers, corn, green beans, and pumpkin, at the peak of their season, plus, of course, meats, seafood, homemade chili, soup, and so on.

This specialized canner has a lid that securely locks in place and a pressure gauge, which allow steam to build up inside the canner and raise the temperature of the water above the boiling point (212°F) to 240°F, killing harmful microorganisms. This is not the same as a pressure cooker, and the two are not interchangeable for canning. There are two types of pressure canners: a weighted-gauge and a dial-gauge. For either, it is important to follow the manufacturer's instructions for use. In addition, if you live at an altitude higher than 1,000 feet above sea level, it is important to consult an altitude adjustment chart for pressure canning. These charts are provided in the manufacturer's instructions.

Dehydrating

Dehydration, or drying, is another form of preserving. In this modern DIY era with Community Supported Agriculture (CSA), farmers' markets, and backyard gardens, preserving food through dehydration makes the pantry feel abundant long after the season's harvest. In this instance, the process involves removing water from foods such as fruits, vegetables, mushrooms, herbs, and in some instances meat and fish. This is an ancient form of preserving, as we think of foods such as fruits, berries, and beans spread on the ground or on racks to dry. In addition, hunters removed the moisture from meat by building fires and heating and smoking their game. Fishers and gatherers, across all cultures, applied the same techniques to preserving seafood and mushrooms—just think of all the dried mushrooms and fish in an Asian market.

Though we dry many foods at home to stock our pantry and give as gifts, in *Gifts Cooks Love*, we focus on prized fresh porcini mushrooms, gathered with a colleague trained in mycology or purchased at the farmers' market, as our gift of choice. The process of drying mushrooms requires minimal preparation—brushing the mushrooms clean, slicing them, and arranging them on trays—and plenty of unattended time as the porcinis dry. Having the right equipment (see page 4), including a food dehydrator with multiple trays, heater, fan to circulate the heat, and temperature control gauge, is the key to success. The gift-giving possibilities and fun begin when you think of all the seasonal food preserving options: dried cherry tomatoes, dried Italian plums, apricots, cherries, fruit leathers, and herbs. Follow the charts and directions provided in the manufacturer's instructions.

CHAPTER 5

SWEET PRESERVED *gifts*

There's something magical about opening a jar of homemade jam or marmalade and slathering the sweet, sassy contents onto a warm piece of brioche—or, better yet, eating it straight from the jar with a spoon! Whether these quick and easy-to-prepare edible indulgences summon nostalgic memories of childhood, a lifelong friendship, or just the perfect cloudless day, your gift recipients will be delighted when you give them these hand-crafted, sweet preserved offerings.

MEYER LEMON CURD

INGREDIENTS

6 large egg yolks, at room temperature

6 large eggs, at room temperature

1½ cups granulated sugar

1 cup freshly squeezed Meyer lemon juice

2 tablespoons grated Meyer lemon zest (from about 3 lemons)

6 tablespoons (¾ stick) unsalted butter, cubed

IMPLEMENTS

Four (½-Pint) Decorative Glass Jars with Tight-Fitting Lids, Medium and Large Bowls, Measuring Cups and Spoons, Cutting Board, Zester, Paring Knife, Juicer, Whisk, Double Boiler, Silicone Spatula, Instant-Read Thermometer, Wide-Mouth Funnel, Ladle

Just try to resist eating this from the jar with a spoon! Pack the lemon curd into jars for gift giving, but save a jar for yourself and spread the lemon curd on toasted brioche or warm-from-the-oven scones. There's enough to fill tiny shortbread tarts or to dollop on an angel food cake served with fresh strawberries. The lemon curd is delightful when layered with raspberries and blueberries for a summertime parfait. Offer all these suggestions on a gift card and, in addition, give a recipe card for Meyer Lemon Mousse, a sneaky-easy and delicious dessert. It's a perfect hostess gift—ready to be enjoyed at breakfast, at teatime, or for dessert.

Prep Time: 20 minutes | Cook Time: 12 to 15 minutes | Makes four (½-pint) jars of lemon curd

1 Wash the jars and lids in hot, soapy water and dry thoroughly. Alternatively, run the jars through the regular cycle of your dishwasher; wash the lids by hand.

2 In a large bowl, whisk together the egg yolks, eggs, and sugar. Whisk in the lemon juice. Transfer to a double boiler. Cook over barely simmering water, whisking constantly, until the lemon mixture thickens and reaches 170°F on an instant-read thermometer. (The mixture will be very foamy on top.)

3 Remove the pan from the heat and whisk in the lemon zest and butter.

4 Using a wide-mouth funnel and filling one jar at a time, ladle the sauce into the prepared jars, leaving ½ inch headspace. Wipe the rims clean. Seal the jars and refrigerate until the lemon curd is thickened and completely cold, at least 4 hours.

MEYER LEMON MOUSSE WITH FRESH BERRIES

Meyer Lemon Curd is tangy and decadent spooned straight from the jar, but resist temptation and try this simple luscious mousse. Transfer all of the lemon curd to a medium bowl. Whip 2 cups of whipping cream along with 3 T. of confectioners' sugar until soft peaks form. Using a rubber spatula, fold a glob of the whipped cream into the lemon curd to lighten it. Gently fold in the rest of the whipped cream. Spoon the mousse into parfait glasses, alternating layers with fresh berries of your choice. Refrigerate until ready to serve. Serves 6 to 8.

STORING: *Refrigerate, covered, for up to 1 week.*

GIFT-GIVING TIPS: Tie each jar with raffia or ribbon and attach a recipe card. To turn this into a gift basket, consider including baked scones, biscuits, or even a loaf of poppy seed cake. For a more elaborate gift, see page 169 for a gift kit idea.

ALEPPO PEPPER–PEACH CHUTNEY

INGREDIENTS

2 tablespoons yellow mustard seeds

4 pounds (8 large) firm but ripe
   freestone peaches

2 cups finely chopped white onion

4 large cloves garlic, minced

2 cups seedless golden raisins

2 cups firmly packed light brown
   sugar

1 cup cider vinegar

2 (3-inch-long) cinnamon sticks

4 teaspoons kosher or sea salt

1 tablespoon ground Aleppo pepper

IMPLEMENTS

Small Sauté Pan, Small Plate,
Large Pot, Large Bowl, Paring Knife,
Slotted Spoon, Cutting Board,
Chef's Knife, Measuring Cups and
Spoons, 6-Quart Saucepan, Silicone
Spatula or Wooden Spoon, Eight
(½-Pint) Glass Canning Jars, Water
Bath Canner, Wide-Mouth Funnel,
Ladle, Wooden Chopstick or Skewer,
Canning Jar Lifter, Kitchen Towel,
Sturdy Rimmed Baking Sheet

Aleppo peppers are a dark red, sweet-and-sharp chile named after the town of Aleppo in northern Syria. They are moderately hot but not overpowering, and they have a fruity quality and almost raisin-like flavor with a touch of salt. Dried and crushed into flakes, Aleppo pepper adds a complex flavor to fish, vegetables, and meats. It's the sweet-and-sharp quality that makes this chutney so intriguingly delicious and a perfect accompaniment to roast or grilled chicken or pork. Preserve the juicy sweetness of peaches at the peak of season, and give this chutney any time of year.

Prep Time: 25 minutes | Cook Time: 1 hour | Processing Time: 10 minutes | Makes eight (½-pint) jars of chutney

1 In a small, dry sauté pan over medium-low heat, toast the mustard seeds by swirling them around in the pan until they release their aroma and take on a slightly darker color, 1 to 2 minutes. Transfer the seeds to a small plate and set aside.

2 Bring a large pot of water to a boil. Have ready a large bowl filled with ice water. Meanwhile, using a paring knife, score the bottom of each peach with a small "x." Working in batches, place the peaches in the boiling water for 30 seconds and then, using a slotted spoon, transfer them to the ice water to cool for 1 minute. Slip off the skins or use a paring knife to help remove any peel adhering to the flesh. Cut the peaches in half, discard the pit, and cut into ¼-inch dice.

3 Combine the peaches, onions, garlic, raisins, sugar, vinegar, cinnamon sticks, salt, and pepper in a deep 6-quart saucepan. Bring to a boil over medium-high heat, stirring occasionally. Decrease to a simmer and cook, uncovered, until the chutney is thick and has a deep golden color, about 50 minutes.

4 While the chutney is simmering, prepare the preserving jars and bring water to a boil in a water bath canner. (See page 7.)

5 Remove the chutney from the heat. Using a wide-mouth funnel and filling one jar at a time, ladle the chutney into hot, sterilized jars, leaving ½ inch headspace. Remove any air bubbles by running a long wooden utensil, such as a chopstick or wooden skewer, between the jar and the chutney. Wipe the rims clean. Seal according to the manufacturer's directions. Process the jars in a boiling water bath for 10 minutes, and then turn off the heat. Wait 5 minutes, and then lift the canning rack and, using a canning jar lifter, transfer the jars to a towel-lined, sturdy rimmed baking sheet and let them rest. Check the seals, wipe the jars, and label.

STORING: *Store the jars in a cool, dark place for up to 1 year.*

GIFT CARD: This preserved Aleppo Pepper–Peach Chutney makes a terrific accompaniment to roast or grilled chicken, can be spooned over crostini spread with fresh goat cheese, or can be mixed with a little mayonnaise to slather on a roast pork or turkey sandwich. The chutney was made on [give date]. Sealed, it will keep for up to 1 year. Once opened, keep refrigerated for up to 3 months. Serve at room temperature.

GIFT-GIVING TIPS: Tie each jar with raffia or ribbon and attach a gift card. To turn this into a gift basket, consider including crackers, fresh goat cheese, and hard salami. For a more elaborate gift, see page 174 for a gift kit idea.

Orange-Cardamom
Marmalade

To: Leslie

ORANGE-CARDAMOM MARMALADE

INGREDIENTS

2½ pounds (6 to 8 medium) oranges, such as Valencia or Cara Cara

¾ pound (about 2 large) lemons

6 cups cold water

20 green cardamom pods, crushed

8 cups granulated sugar

IMPLEMENTS

Cutting Board, Paring Knife, Small Container with Lid, Chef's Knife or Mandoline, 6-Quart Saucepan, Measuring Cups, Silicone Spatula, Cheesecloth, Kitchen Twine, Eleven (½-Pint) Glass Canning Jars with Lids and Screw Bands, Water Bath Canner, Candy Thermometer, Wide-Mouth Funnel, Ladle, Wooden Chopstick or Skewer, Canning Jar Lifter, Kitchen Towel, Sturdy Rimmed Baking Sheet

We tend to think of preserving and canning as a summertime activity, and rightfully so, with all the luscious berries and stone fruits in season; however, in winter, with the new crop of citrus in the market, the timing is perfect for putting up marmalade and giving it as gifts for the holidays. Select blemish-free citrus, preferably organically grown, because for marmalade you use the fruit's skin, pith, and flesh. The pith is naturally high in pectin, as are the seeds, which is why they are reserved, tied in a cheesecloth bag, and cooked along with the fruit. Cardamom is an aromatic spice that delicately perfumes the marmalade and adds a spicy-sweet flavor. The crushed cardamom pods and seeds are added to the bag containing the citrus seeds, so they can easily be removed once the marmalade is done. Look for green cardamom at an Indian grocer or in a specialty store, or order it online from a spice company such as Penzeys Spices (www.penzeys.com).

Prep Time: 20 minutes | Soaking Time: 12 to 24 hours | Cook Time: about 1 hour | Processing Time: 10 minutes | Makes eleven (½-pint) jars of marmalade

1 Prepare the fruit 12 to 24 hours before you plan to cook and preserve the marmalade. Wash and pat dry all the fruit. Trim and discard the stem ends. Cut the oranges and lemons into quarters and poke out all the seeds with the tip of a paring knife. Reserve the seeds in a small covered container. Using a sharp chef's knife or mandoline, cut all the citrus, including the rinds, into $\frac{1}{16}$-inch-thick slices. Put the sliced fruit in a large pot, including any juices left on the cutting board. Add the 6 cups of water. Gently press down on the fruit to make sure it is submerged. Cover the pot and set aside at room temperature for 12 to 24 hours. (This softens the rinds and releases the pectin.)

2   The next day, bring the pot of sliced fruit and water to a boil over medium-high heat. Adjust the heat so the mixture boils steadily without splattering, and cook for 30 minutes. Wrap the crushed cardamom pods and the reserved lemon and orange seeds in a cheesecloth bag tied securely with kitchen twine.

3   While the fruit is cooking, prepare the preserving jars and bring water to a boil in a water bath canner. (See page 7.) Sterilize the jars and lids. (See page 29.)

4   Add the sugar to the fruit mixture and stir until dissolved. Add the cheesecloth bag of cardamom and seeds. Continue to cook the marmalade at a steady boil until it reaches the gel stage (see Note) or reaches 220°F on a candy thermometer, 30 to 40 minutes longer.

5   Remove the cheesecloth bag from the marmalade, pressing any liquids back into the pan.

6   Remove the marmalade from the heat. Using a wide-mouth funnel and filling one jar at a time, ladle the marmalade into hot, sterilized jars, leaving ½ inch headspace. Remove any air bubbles by running a long wooden utensil, such as a chopstick or wooden skewer, between the jar and the marmalade. Wipe the rims clean. Seal according to the manufacturer's directions. Process the jars in a boiling water bath for 10 minutes, and then turn off the heat. Wait 5 minutes, and then lift the canning rack and, using a canning jar lifter, transfer the jars to a towel-lined, sturdy rimmed baking sheet and let them rest. Check the seals, wipe the jars, and label.

Note: Here's an easy way to check whether the marmalade is set. Put a small plate in the freezer. When the marmalade looks thickish and a bit gelled, put a small amount of the marmalade on the frozen plate and return it to the freezer. After a couple of minutes, run your finger or a spoon down the center and see if it stays separated and is a bit wrinkled. If so, it is done.

STORING: *Store the jars in a cool, dark place for up to 1 year.*

GIFT CARD: This preserved Orange-Cardamom Marmalade can be spooned over buttered toast, spread on a brioche roll or croissant, or dolloped on a toasted English muffin spread with fresh goat cheese. The marmalade was made on [give date]. Sealed, it will keep for up to 1 year. Once opened, keep refrigerated for up to 6 months.

GIFT-GIVING TIPS: Tie each jar with raffia or ribbon and attach a gift card. To turn this into a gift basket, consider including some fresh goat cheese and English muffins, or a loaf of brioche or artisan bread for toasting. To make the gift a bit more elaborate, wrap the marmalade and bread and place in a tea towel–lined bread basket and include a butter spreader, if desired; or see page 169 for a gift kit idea.

BOYSENBERRY AND LEMON VERBENA JAM

INGREDIENTS

4 pounds (9 cups) fresh
   boysenberries

2 cups granulated sugar

24 large fresh lemon verbena leaves

IMPLEMENTS

Measuring Cups, 6-Quart Saucepan, Silicone Spatula, Spice or Coffee Grinder or Mini Food Processor, Six (½-Pint) Glass Canning Jars with Lids and Screw Bands, Water Bath Canner, Potato Masher or Large Metal Spoon, Ladle, Fine-Mesh Strainer, Medium Bowl, Wide-Mouth Funnel, Wooden Chopstick or Skewer, Canning Jar Lifter, Kitchen Towel, Sturdy Rimmed Baking Sheet

With big berry taste and lemony herbal notes, this vibrant jam is a delicious twist on traditional boysenberry spreads. It took many trials and test batches to figure out the best way to capture the bright herbal essence of fresh lemon verbena in this jam. Placing the whole leaves in a cheesecloth bag and cooking them along with the fruit diminished the flavor, as did mincing the leaves; however, when the leaves are pulverized along with sugar in a spice or coffee grinder, the oils cling to the sugar. Adding the sugar during the last 5 minutes of cooking is just enough time to dissolve the sugar and perfume the fruit. Be sure your spice or coffee grinder is absolutely clean; if not, clean it by adding a few spoonfuls of uncooked white rice and grinding it to a fine powder. Tap out the rice powder, wipe the inside, and proceed to make the lemon verbena sugar.

Prep Time: 10 minutes | Resting Time: 30 minutes | Cook Time: about 25 minutes | Processing Time: 10 minutes | Makes six (½-pint) jars of jam

1 Combine the boysenberries and 1¾ cups of the sugar in a large pot. Mix well and set aside for 30 minutes to allow the berries to release some of their juices.

2 Meanwhile, in a clean spice or coffee grinder or mini food processor, process the remaining ¼ cup of sugar and lemon verbena leaves until finely ground. Set aside.

3 Wash the jars, including the lids and screw bands, in hot, soapy water. Alternatively, run the jars through the regular cycle of your dishwasher; wash the lids and screw bands by hand. Bring water to a boil in a water bath canner. (See page 7.)

4 Place the pot with the berry mixture over medium-high heat and bring to a simmer. Decrease the heat so the mixture simmers slowly without splattering, and cook for 15 minutes. Use a potato masher or the back of a metal spoon to break down the berries.

5 Using a ladle and working in batches, transfer about 4 cups of the berry mixture to a fine-mesh strainer set over a bowl. Using a silicone spatula, press the mixture through the strainer to extract the seeds. Discard the seeds. Return the strained berry mixture to the pot and bring to a simmer over medium-high heat. Skim any foam from the surface and cook for 5 minutes.

6 Add the lemon verbena sugar, stir to dissolve the sugar, and cook 5 minutes longer.

7 Remove the jam from the heat. Using a wide-mouth funnel and filling one jar at a time, ladle the jam into hot, sterilized jars, leaving ½ inch headspace. Remove any air bubbles by running a long wooden utensil, such as a chopstick or wooden skewer, between the jar and the jam. Wipe the rims clean. Seal according to the manufacturer's directions. Process the jars in a boiling water bath for 10 minutes, and then turn off the heat. Wait 5 minutes, and then lift the canning rack and, using a canning jar lifter, transfer the jars to a towel-lined, sturdy rimmed baking sheet and let them rest. Check the seals, wipe the jars, and label.

STORING: *Store the jars in a cool, dark place for up to 1 year.*

GIFT CARD: This Boysenberry and Lemon Verbena Jam can be spooned over buttered toast, spread on a brioche roll or croissant, or dolloped on a toasted English muffin spread with butter or fresh goat cheese. The jam was made on [give date]. Sealed, it will keep for up to 1 year. Once opened, keep refrigerated for up to 6 months.

GIFT-GIVING TIPS: Tie each jar with raffia or ribbon and attach a gift card. To turn this into a gift basket, consider including some imported unsalted butter and a loaf of brioche or artisan bread for toasting. To make the gift a bit more elaborate, soften the butter and pack into a porcelain butter keeper, and then wrap the jam, butter, and bread in a tea towel–lined bread basket and include a jam spoon, if desired; or see page 169 for a gift kit idea.

CINNAMON-SPICED CRABAPPLES

INGREDIENTS

1 (3-inch-long) cinnamon stick

3 whole star anise

1 tablespoon whole cloves

2 teaspoons black peppercorns

4½ cups granulated sugar

3 cups water

2½ cups cider vinegar

2 pounds (about 8 cups) crabapples

IMPLEMENTS

Four or Five (1-Pint/½-Liter) Glass Canning Jars, Water Bath Canner, Measuring Cups and Spoons, Kitchen Shears, Cheesecloth, Kitchen Twine, 6-Quart Saucepan, Silicone Spatula, Wooden or Metal Skewer, Slotted Spoon, Wide-Mouth Funnel, Ladle, Wooden Chopstick or Skewer, Canning Jar Lifter, Sturdy Rimmed Baking Sheet

This recipe will be ideal for the cook with a crabapple tree in the yard or in a friend's yard! However, during the fall months, you'll also often see crabapples for sale at farmers' markets. These small, adorable, blushed-red apples are too hard and tart to eat out of hand, but they make incredible jams and jellies. My favorite way to preserve them is to pack them into jars whole and then fill the jar with a spice-infused, sweet pickling liquid. Once processed, these rosy orbs are suspended in a transparent, pink-tinged liquid—delectably cute and wonderful for gift giving. They are perfect with charcuterie and make a terrific accompaniment to roast pork and poultry.

Prep Time: 25 minutes | Cook Time: 18 minutes | Processing Time: 20 minutes | Makes four to five (1-pint/½-liter) jars of crabapples

1 Wash the jars, including the lids and screw bands, in hot, soapy water. Alternatively, run the jars through the regular cycle of your dishwasher; wash the lids and screw bands by hand. Bring water to a boil in a water bath canner. (See page 7.) Sterilize the jars and lids. (See page 29.)

2 Place the cinnamon stick, star anise, cloves, and peppercorns on a square of cheesecloth and tie securely with kitchen twine to form a spice bag.

3 In a 6-quart saucepan, combine the sugar, water, and vinegar. Bring to a boil over high heat, stirring until the sugar is dissolved. Add the spice bag. Decrease the heat to low, cover, and simmer for 15 minutes.

4 Meanwhile, wash the crabapples and pat dry with paper towels. Using kitchen shears, snip the stem ends, leaving ½ inch intact. Using a skewer, prick each crabapple in several places. Set aside. (This allows the spiced syrup to permeate the crabapples and reduces the amount of bursting when the fruit is heated.)

5 Add the crabapples to the pot and simmer, uncovered, for 3 minutes.

6 Using a slotted spoon and wide-mouth funnel, pack the crabapples into the hot, sterilized jars, leaving a generous ½ inch headspace. Ladle the hot syrup into the jars, covering the crabapples and leaving ½ inch headspace. Remove any air bubbles by running a long wooden utensil, such as a chopstick or wooden skewer, between the jar and the syrup. Wipe the rims clean. Seal according to the manufacturer's directions. Process the jars in a boiling water bath for 20 minutes, and then turn off the heat. Wait 5 minutes, and then lift the canning rack and, using a canning jar lifter, transfer the jars to a sturdy rimmed baking sheet lined with a double thickness of paper towels and let them rest. (Use paper towels rather than a cloth kitchen towel because the liquids might weep a bit and turn the cloth pink.) Check the seals, wipe the jars, and label.

STORING: *Store the jars in a cool, dark place for up to 1 year.*

GIFT CARD: These Cinnamon-Spiced Crabapples are a perfect accompaniment to roast chicken and turkey, and they complement roast pork as well. Serve them at your holiday meal in place of the traditional cranberry sauce. The crabapples were made on [give date]. Sealed, they will keep for up to 1 year. Once opened, keep refrigerated for up to 3 months.

GIFT-GIVING TIPS: Tie each jar with raffia or ribbon and attach a gift card. To turn this into a gift basket, consider including a package of wild rice, dry-roasted nuts, and some dried fruits—all possible ingredients for a wild rice stuffing to accompany a holiday bird.

CHAPTER 6

SAVORY PRESERVED *gifts*

Chutneys, compotes, and flavored mustards are the new staples *du jour* of any cook's pantry. Cooks often have their pantry chockablock with chutneys that get used frequently to "dress up" weeknight meals. How wonderful, then, to preserve your own bounty, artfully present it to a friend, and provide a tasty, versatile accompaniment for days and weeks to come. So give the gift that keeps on giving *and* add a beautiful, jewel-toned accent to any menu at any time of year.

EIGHT-HOUR BUTTER-BRAISED ONIONS

INGREDIENTS

10 large (about 8½ pounds) sweet
  onions, such as Walla Walla,
  Vidalia, or Maui
½ cup (1 stick) unsalted butter,
  thinly sliced
2 tablespoons minced fresh thyme

IMPLEMENTS

Onion Goggles, Cutting Board,
Chef's Knife, 6½-Quart Electric
Slow Cooker, Measuring Spoon,
Silicone Spatula, Two (6-Cup/
1½-Liter) Glass, Canning Jars,
Wide-Mouth Funnel, Ladle

Onions as a gift? Indeed. This is the perfect hostess gift when the invitation to a friend's cabin for a ski weekend arrives. Bring along the makings for an après-ski lunch of French onion soup. Requiring only a slow cooker and a little attention from the cook, the preparation is nearly done before the trip. Thick slices of onion are simmered for hours in butter and fresh thyme until meltingly soft and savory. This becomes the base for the classic and hearty soup, served piping hot with melted Gruyère bubbling over toasted bread and oozing down the sides of a ceramic bowl. Pack an artisan loaf of bread, a hunk of cheese, and a bottle of Beaujolais, and you are in winter heaven.

Prep Time: 20 minutes | Cook Time: 8 hours | Makes two (6-cup/1½-liter) jars of butter-braised onions; enough for two batches of French onion soup, six servings each

1 To prep the onions, trim the stem end, cut in half lengthwise through the root, and peel each half. Leaving the root end intact, cut each half lengthwise into ¼-inch-thick slices. Trim to remove the root.

2 Scatter the butter in the bottom of a 6½-quart electric slow cooker. Add the onions and sprinkle the thyme over the top. Place the lid on the slow cooker, set the cooking mode to high, and set a timer for 2 hours.

3 After 2 hours, use a silicone spatula to stir the onion mixture. Set a timer for 6 hours, continuing to cook on high. (As tempting as it might be, there is no need to stir the onions during this long cooking period.)

4 Turn the power off, remove the cover, give the onions a stir, and let cool in the ceramic insert for 1 hour.

5 Ladle the onions into the jars through a wide-mouth funnel, dividing evenly. Cool completely, and then cover and refrigerate.

RECIPE CARD: CREATE A CARD TO PACKAGE WITH GIFT

BISTRO-STYLE FRENCH ONION SOUP

In a large saucepan over medium heat, melt 1½ T. of unsalted butter. Add 1½ T. of all-purpose flour, and whisk until the flour is absorbed and begins to turn golden. Add 1 T. of sugar; whisk to dissolve. Add the onions and 4 cups of chicken broth. Bring to a simmer. Season to taste. Have ready 6 thick slices of toasted French bread and 6 thick slices of Gruyère cheese. Divide the soup among 6 heatproof bowls, and top with a slice of bread and cheese. Place on a rimmed baking sheet. Broil until the cheese is melted and bubbling. Serve immediately. Serves 6.

STORING: *Refrigerate, covered, for up to 5 days.*

GIFT-GIVING TIPS: Tie each jar with raffia or ribbon and attach a recipe card. To turn this into a gift basket, consider including an artisan loaf of bread and a hunk of Gruyère cheese. To make the gift a bit more elaborate, include 6 French onion soup bowls.

GREEN TOMATO CHUTNEY

INGREDIENTS

4 pounds green tomatoes,
  cored and coarsely chopped

1½ pounds (2 medium) yellow
  onions, chopped

1 pound (2 large) firm, tart green
  apples, cored and chopped

6 large cloves garlic

2½ cups cider vinegar

2½ cups firmly packed light
  brown sugar

⅓ cup honey

1½ tablespoons mustard seeds

1 tablespoon kosher or sea salt

2 teaspoons ground ginger

2 teaspoons ground allspice

5 fresh medium-hot red chiles,
  with seeds and ribs, thinly
  sliced into rounds

¾ cup dried currants

IMPLEMENTS

Cutting Board, Paring Knife, Chef's
Knife, Measuring Cups and Spoons,
10-Quart Dutch Oven, Wooden
Spoon, Six (1-Pint/½-Liter) Glass
Canning Jars, Water Bath Canner,
Wide-Mouth Funnel, Ladle, Wooden
Chopstick or Skewer, Canning
Jar Lifter, Kitchen Towel, Sturdy
Rimmed Baking Sheet

Cherokee Green, Green Giant, or even the smaller Green Zebra heirloom tomatoes are lovely to look at and luscious to eat, but these are not the tomatoes used to make this fabulous end-of-summer chutney. Rather, seek out the orphaned, firm, and completely underripe tomatoes that hang on the vines in every gardener's vegetable patch, for they are the desired tomatoes for this recipe. With fresh chiles and early fall apples also peaking at this time of year, this chutney is a seasonal delight to share with friends. Choose fresh chiles that deliver a real heat kick, or make milder-flavored chutney by using red-skinned Anaheim chiles.

Prep Time: 25 minutes | Cook Time: 1 to 1¼ hours | Processing Time: 10 minutes | Makes six (1-pint/½-liter) jars of chutney

1 Combine the tomatoes, onions, apples, garlic, vinegar, sugar, honey, mustard seeds, salt, ginger, and allspice in a large Dutch oven. Bring to a boil over medium-high heat, stirring occasionally. Decrease to a simmer and cook, uncovered, for 30 minutes. As the mixture simmers, use a wooden spoon to push down the tomatoes so they become immersed in the liquid.

2 Add the chiles and currants and continue to simmer until the chutney is thick and the liquid is reduced, 30 to 45 minutes longer.

3 While the chutney is simmering, prepare the preserving jars and bring water to a boil in a water bath canner. (See page 7.)

4 Remove the chutney from the heat. Using a wide-mouth funnel and filling one jar at a time, ladle the chutney into hot, sterilized jars, leaving ½ inch headspace. Remove any air bubbles by running a long wooden utensil, such as a chopstick or wooden skewer, between the jar and the chutney. Wipe the rims clean. Seal according to the manufacturer's directions. Process the jars in a boiling water bath for 10 minutes, and then turn off the heat. Wait 5 minutes, and then lift the canning rack and, using a canning jar lifter, transfer the jars to a towel-lined, sturdy rimmed baking sheet and let them rest. Check the seals, wipe the jars, and label.

STORING: *Store the jars in a cool, dark place for up to 1 year.*

GIFT CARD: This preserved Green Tomato Chutney is tangy, with a real kick of spice. It makes a terrific accompaniment to roast chicken, can be spooned over crostini spread with fresh goat cheese, or can be mixed with a little mayonnaise to slather on a roast pork or turkey sandwich. The chutney was made on [give date]. Sealed, it will keep for up to 1 year. Once opened, keep refrigerated for up to 3 months. Serve at room temperature.

GIFT-GIVING TIPS: Tie each jar with raffia or ribbon and attach a gift card. To turn this into a gift basket, consider including crackers, aged or smoked Gouda, or a fresh goat cheese. To make the gift a bit more elaborate, see page 166 for a gift kit idea.

green tomato
chutney

green tomato
chutney

PICKLED CHERRIES WITH SAVORY AND SPICE

INGREDIENTS

3 pounds fresh dark cherries, such
　　as Bing, Van, Lambert, or Stella

12 (4-inch) sprigs fresh savory

4 cups white wine vinegar

2 cups water

2 cups granulated sugar

1½ tablespoons black peppercorns

2 whole star anise

2 fresh bay leaves, torn

IMPLEMENTS

Three (1-Quart/1-Liter) Glass
Canning Jars, Colander, Kitchen
Shears, Rounded Wooden Skewer
or Toothpick, Measuring Cups and
Spoons, 3-Quart Saucepan, Wooden
Spoon or Silicone Spatula, Wide-
Mouth Funnel, Ladle

Cherry season is greatly anticipated and yet so fleeting.
There are only so many you can eat out of hand, top with
a buttery and sweet nut crust for a crisp, or tumble with
a little sugar and cornstarch to bake into a flaky pie. To
truly savor and preserve the season, pack fresh cherries
into hinged-top French canning jars and pickle them for a
spiced, tart accompaniment to pâtés, game meats, seared
duck breasts, or pork roasts.

Prep Time: 30 minutes | Cook Time: 10 minutes | Pickling Time: 2 weeks |
Makes three (1-quart/1-liter) jars of pickled cherries

1　Wash the jars, including the lids and screw bands, in hot, soapy
　　water and dry thoroughly. Alternatively, run the jars through
　　the regular cycle of your dishwasher; wash the lids and screw
　　bands by hand. Sterilize the jars and lids. (See page 29.)

2　Wash the cherries and pat dry with paper towels. Using kitchen
　　shears, snip the stem ends, leaving ¾ inch intact. Using a
　　skewer or toothpick, prick each cherry in several places. (This
　　allows the pickling liquid to permeate into the cherry.) Fill the
　　jars half full of cherries.

3　Nestle 4 sprigs of savory into each jar, spacing them evenly
　　down the sides of the jars. Fill the jars evenly with the rest of
　　the cherries.

4　In a 3-quart saucepan, combine the vinegar, water, sugar,
　　peppercorns, star anise, and bay leaves. Bring to a boil over
　　high heat, stirring constantly until the sugar dissolves. Boil the
　　pickling liquid for 1 minute and remove from the heat.

5   Using a wide-mouth funnel, ladle the hot pickling liquid into the prepared jars filled with cherries, covering the fruit and leaving ½ inch headspace. Wipe the rims clean and attach the lids. Steep at room temperature until cool. Store in the refrigerator for 2 weeks to allow the flavors to permeate the cherries.

STORING: *Refrigerate, covered, for 2 weeks and up to 6 months.*

GIFT CARD: These hand-crafted Pickled Cherries with Savory and Spice were made on [give date] and can be enjoyed for up to 6 months. Keep refrigerated, but serve at room temperature. They make a delightful accompaniment to charcuterie, pâté, and smoked fish.

GIFT-GIVING TIPS: Tie each jar with raffia or ribbon and attach a gift card. To turn this into a gift basket, consider including some chicken liver pâté or a selection of charcuterie along with a jar of whole-grain mustard and store-bought or homemade crackers (see page 111). These pickled cherries are equally delicious with smoked or cured salmon (see page 77).

APRICOT-BOURBON MUSTARD

INGREDIENTS

⅔ cup yellow mustard seeds

1 cup bourbon, such as Maker's
   Mark

⅔ cup water

⅔ cup packed chopped dried
   apricots

4 tablespoons cider vinegar

4 tablespoons honey

1 tablespoon kosher or sea salt

IMPLEMENTS

Measuring Cups and Spoons, Two
Medium Bowls, Cutting Board,
Chef's Knife, Four (6-Ounce)
Condiment Jars, Strainer, Rubber
Spatula, Food Processor

Do you have a Dagwood-style sandwich maker on your gift list, one of those friends or a family member who loves nothing more than raiding the refrigerator and making a mile-high sandwich layered with meats and cheese and smeared with mayonnaise and mustard? This is the perfect gift—a unique homemade mustard blending the sweetness of dried apricots steeped in bourbon with the bright bite of whole mustard seeds.

Soak Time: 12 to 24 hours | Prep Time: 20 minutes | Maturation Time: 2 weeks | Makes 2⅔ cups, enough to fill four (6-ounce) condiment jars

1 Put the mustard seeds in a medium bowl and pour in ⅔ cup of the bourbon and the water. Soak the mustard seeds overnight or for up to 24 hours.

2 At least 1 hour before you plan to make the mustard, put the apricots in a bowl and pour in the remaining ⅓ cup bourbon. Macerate the apricots until most of the bourbon is absorbed. (The apricots need to soak for a minimum of 1 hour, or you can start soaking them at the same time you prepare the mustard seeds.)

3 Before making the mustard, wash the jars and lids in hot, soapy water and dry thoroughly. Alternatively, run the jars through the regular cycle of your dishwasher.

4 To make the mustard, first strain the mustard seeds, reserving the soaking liquid. Set aside the mustard seeds.

5 In a food processor fitted with the metal blade, combine the apricots, any unabsorbed bourbon remaining in the bowl, cider vinegar, honey, and salt. Purée until almost smooth. Add the mustard seed soaking liquid and continue to purée until smooth. Add the mustard seeds and process until about half of the seeds are cracked and the others are incorporated but still whole.

6 Evenly divide the mustard among the prepared condiment jars, leaving ½ inch headspace. Wipe the rims clean and secure the lids. Label and refrigerate for at least 2 weeks to allow the flavors to develop and mature.

STORING: *Refrigerate for a minimum of 2 weeks and up to 3 months.*

GIFT CARD: This Apricot-Bourbon Mustard was made on [give date] and can be enjoyed for up to 3 months, kept in the refrigerator. It makes a delightful sandwich spread and a great dip for hard or soft-baked pretzels, or use it as a condiment for cured meats and smoked or grilled sausages.

GIFT-GIVING TIPS: Tie each jar with raffia or ribbon and attach a gift card. To turn this into a gift basket, consider including a bag of twisted hard pretzels, or smoked sausages, cured meats, crackers, and a jar of cornichons.

apricot bourbo mustard

Arrabbiata Sauce

ARRABBIATA SAUCE

INGREDIENTS

8 pounds fresh, ripe Roma, plum, or
  San Marzano tomatoes

½ cup extra-virgin olive oil

2 large yellow onions, finely diced
  (about 4 cups)

½ cup minced serrano chiles,
  including seeds and ribs

8 large cloves garlic, minced

1 (12-ounce) can tomato paste

3 tablespoons granulated sugar

2 tablespoons kosher or sea salt

½ teaspoon freshly ground black
  pepper

1½ teaspoons citric acid, such as
  Fruit-Fresh

IMPLEMENTS

Stockpot, Large Bowl, Paring Knife,
Cutting Board, Slotted Spoon, Chef's
Knife, Measuring Cups and Spoons,
Silicone Spatula, Can Opener, Six
(1-Pint/½-Liter) Glass Canning Jars,
Water Bath Canner, Wide-Mouth
Funnel, Ladle, Wooden Chopstick or
Skewer, Canning Jar Lifter, Kitchen
Towel, Sturdy Rimmed Baking Sheet

Arrabbiata means "angry" in Italian and refers to the chile-infused piquancy of this sauce. It is a dynamite way to use fresh-from-the-farmers'-market (or garden-picked) plum or Roma tomatoes. Buy yourself some disposable surgical gloves at the pharmacy and wear them when working with chiles. They will keep the caustic compound (capsaicin) that is naturally present in chiles from irritating your skin.

Prep Time: 30 minutes | Cook Time: 40 minutes | Processing Time: 40 minutes | Makes six (1-pint/½-liter) jars of arrabbiata sauce

1 Bring a large pot of water to a boil. Have ready a large bowl filled with ice water. Meanwhile, using a paring knife, score the pointed end of each tomato with a small "x." Working in batches, place the tomatoes in the boiling water for 30 seconds and then, using a slotted spoon, transfer them to the ice water to cool for 1 minute. Use a paring knife to peel back the skins and remove the cores. Coarsely chop the tomatoes, transfer to a bowl, and set aside.

2 In a large stockpot over medium-high heat, warm the olive oil and swirl to coat the pan. Add the onions and sauté, stirring frequently, until soft but not brown, about 5 minutes.

3 Add the serrano chiles and garlic and sauté 1 to 2 minutes longer. Do not let the chiles or garlic brown. Add the tomato paste and stir constantly for 1 minute.

4 Add the tomatoes, sugar, salt, and pepper and stir to incorporate. Bring to a boil, adjust the heat so the sauce just simmers, cover, and cook, stirring occasionally, until the tomatoes are no longer chunky and the sauce is thick, about 30 minutes.

5 While the sauce is simmering, prepare the preserving jars and bring water to a boil in a water bath canner. (See page 7.)

6 Remove the sauce from the heat. Using a wide-mouth funnel and filling one jar at a time, ladle the sauce into the hot, sterilized jars, leaving ½ inch headspace. Remove any air bubbles by running a long wooden utensil, such as a chopstick or wooden skewer, between the jar and the sauce. Wipe the rims clean. Seal according to the manufacturer's directions. Process the jars in a boiling water bath for 40 minutes, and then turn off the heat. Wait 5 minutes, and then lift the canning rack and, using a canning jar lifter, transfer the jars to a towel-lined, sturdy rimmed baking sheet and let them rest. Check the seals, wipe the jars, and label.

RECIPE CARD: CREATE A CARD TO PACKAGE WITH GIFT

PENNE WITH ARRABBIATA SAUCE AND BOCCONCINI

Drain 1 cup bocconcini (small fresh mozzarella balls) and set aside. Heat the sauce in a medium sauté pan. Meanwhile, cook 8 ounces of penne according to package directions. Drain, but do not rinse the pasta. Toss the pasta with the sauce and the bocconcini. Heat through. Divide among heated pasta bowls and shower the pasta with freshly grated Parmigiano-Reggiano cheese. Serves 2 to 3.

STORING: *Store the jars in a cool, dark place for up to 1 year.*

GIFT-GIVING TIPS: Tie each jar with raffia or ribbon and attach a recipe card. To turn this into a gift basket, consider including a package of dried artisanal penne pasta and a hunk of Parmigiano-Reggiano cheese. To make the gift a bit more elaborate, see page 170 for a gift kit idea.

CÔTES DU RHÔNE–RHUBARB COMPOTE

INGREDIENTS

4 cups thickly sliced fresh rhubarb, ends trimmed

1 pound firm but ripe Bosc pears, peeled, cored, and cut into ½-inch dice

2 tablespoons finely diced shallots

1½ cups Côtes du Rhône dry red wine

2 tablespoons honey

2 (3-inch-long) cinnamon sticks

¼ teaspoon ground cloves

¾ teaspoon kosher or sea salt

¾ teaspoon freshly ground black pepper

IMPLEMENTS

Cutting Board, Chef's Knife, Vegetable Peeler, Measuring Cups and Spoons, 4-Quart Saucepan, Silicone Spatula or Wooden Spoon, Four (½-Pint) Glass Canning Jars, Water Bath Canner, Wide-Mouth Funnel, Ladle, Wooden Chopstick or Skewer, Canning Jar Lifter, Kitchen Towel, Sturdy Rimmed Baking Sheet

We know that spring has arrived when we see the long ruby-hued stalks of fresh rhubarb at the farmers' market. As simple to work with as a rib of celery, the stalks are cut crosswise into slices after the tops and fibrous bottoms are lopped off. What isn't obvious from rhubarb's crunchy, firm texture is how quickly it cooks down into a rosy purée. It needs sweetness and spice to make it nice, in fact delectable, and this recipe produces a luscious compote, combining the spice and herbiness of Provençal red wine with ripe Bosc pears, a hint of shallot, honey, and cinnamon. Make this a springtime gift to a cook who loves to roast duck, grill pork, or serve a country-style terrine.

Prep Time: 20 minutes | Cook Time: 40 minutes | Processing Time: 10 minutes | Makes about four (½-pint) jars of compote

1 In a 4-quart saucepan over medium heat, combine the rhubarb, pears, shallots, wine, honey, cinnamon sticks, cloves, salt, and pepper. Bring the mixture to a boil. Decrease the heat so the compote is at a low simmer. Cook, stirring frequently, until the rhubarb is completely tender and falling apart, the pears are soft, and the compote has thickened, about 40 minutes. (Use the side of a spoon or silicone spatula to mash any remaining chunks of rhubarb.)

2 While the compote is simmering, prepare the preserving jars and bring water to a boil in a water bath canner. (See page 7.)

3 Remove the compote from the heat. Using a wide-mouth funnel and filling one jar at a time, ladle the compote into hot, sterilized jars, leaving ½ inch headspace. Remove any air bubbles by running a long wooden utensil, such as a chopstick or wooden skewer, between the jar and the compote. Wipe the rims clean. Seal according to the manufacturer's directions. Process the jars in a boiling water bath for 10 minutes, and then turn off the heat. Wait 5 minutes, and then lift the canning rack and, using a canning jar lifter, transfer the jars to a towel-lined, sturdy rimmed baking sheet and let them rest. Check the seals, wipe the jars, and label.

STORING: *Store the jars in a cool, dark place for up to 1 year.*

GIFT CARD: This preserved Côtes du Rhône–Rhubarb Compote is a springtime favorite served as an accompaniment to fresh duck breasts that are seared rare and served fanned on the plate with juice from the pan. It is also a perfect condiment for a country pork terrine, duck confit, or grilled pork tenderloin.

GIFT-GIVING TIPS: Tie each jar with raffia or ribbon and attach a gift card. To turn this into a gift basket, consider including some duck confit, slices of a country pork terrine, and an artisan loaf of bread. For a more elaborate gift, see page 174 for a gift kit idea.

CHAPTER 7

SMOKED, CURED
& DRIED *gifts*

Beware: When they unwrap these unexpected homemade culinary delicacies, the recipients of these food gifts will insist on being your best friends forever! Some gifts are expected (the obligatory bottle of wine comes immediately to mind); some are feared (the much-maligned holiday fruitcake, for example). But homemade ketchup, bacon, and dried mushrooms, among other glorious offerings, pack a walloping surprise.

SMOKY TOMATO KETCHUP

INGREDIENTS

2 tablespoons pulverized apple wood smoking chips

1 medium yellow onion, cut into ½-inch-thick rounds

1 (28-ounce) can crushed tomatoes, including the juice from the can

1 tablespoon capers, drained and rinsed

½ cup firmly packed light brown sugar

Juice of 1 orange, strained

Juice of ½ grapefruit, strained

Juice of ½ lemon, strained

¼ cup cider vinegar

2½ teaspoons kosher or sea salt

¼ teaspoon freshly ground black pepper

IMPLEMENTS

Stovetop Smoker or Wok, Measuring Cups and Spoons, Chef's Knife, Cutting Board, Can Opener, Blender, Heatproof Silicone Spatula, Deep 6-Quart Saucepan or Dutch Oven, Juicer, Three (8-Ounce) Glass Bottles, Narrow-Neck Funnel, Ladle

It's hard to believe I would make my own ketchup to give as gifts considering that I grew up in Pittsburgh, PA—home of Heinz and the big "Heinz 57"sign boldly lit and dominant on the skyline. It never even occurred to me that ketchup could be homemade until I ate at Paley's Place Bistro and Bar in Portland, Oregon, and had chef Vitaly Paley's deliciously nuanced ketchup. He makes all his condiments from scratch, including his ketchup, and I was inspired to make my own. I wanted the bright, fresh flavors of Vitaly's ketchup but with a smoky twist, so with his advice I smoked the onions before stewing them with the tomatoes. Given in old-fashioned, hinge-topped, clear glass bottles, these make an adorable summertime present for the host of a backyard barbecue or as part of a Father's Day gift.

Prep Time: 20 minutes | Smoking Time: 10 minutes | Cook Time: 1 hour | Makes three (8-ounce) bottles of ketchup

1 Using a stovetop smoker or wok, place the wood chips in two small piles in the center of the pan. If using a smoker, place a drip tray, covered with aluminum foil, on top of the chips. If using a wok, set a large sheet of aluminum foil loosely in place over the wood chips. Place a wire rack on top of the drip tray or foil. Arrange the onion slices on the wire rack. Slide the lid on the stovetop smoker or cover the wok, leaving it slightly open, and then place the smoker over medium heat. When the first wisp of smoke appears, close the lid. Smoke the onions for 5 minutes, then turn off the heat and leave the onions in the smoker or wok, with the lid tightly closed, for an additional 5 minutes. Remove the onions from the smoker and coarsely chop.

2 Purée the tomatoes in a blender on high speed until liquefied, about 2 minutes. Transfer the tomatoes to a deep 6-quart saucepan or Dutch oven and reserve.

3 Purée the onions and capers in the blender on high speed for 1 minute. Add the sugar and continue blending on high speed until the onion mixture is smooth, about 1 minute longer. Add the citrus juices, vinegar, salt, and pepper and blend to incorporate. Transfer the onion mixture to the pot with the tomatoes and stir to combine.

4 Over medium heat, bring the tomato and onion mixture to a simmer. Decrease the heat to maintain a low simmer, and cook, stirring occasionally, until the sauce thickens to a ketchup consistency, 50 minutes to 1 hour.

5 While the ketchup is simmering, wash the bottles in hot, soapy water and dry thoroughly. Alternatively, run the bottles through the regular cycle of your dishwasher.

6 Using a funnel, ladle the ketchup into the prepared bottles, leaving ½ inch headspace. Wipe the rims clean and secure the lids. Label and refrigerate.

STORING: *Refrigerate for up to 2 months.*

GIFT CARD: This Smoky Tomato Ketchup was made on [give date] and can be enjoyed for up to 1 month, kept in the refrigerator. It makes a delightful sauce to top meatloaf, hamburgers, or grilled hot dogs, of course.

GIFT-GIVING TIPS: Tie each jar with raffia or ribbon and attach a gift card. To turn this into a gift basket, consider including Apricot-Bourbon Mustard (page 59), pickle relish, all-beef hot dogs, and bakery-fresh buns. For a more elaborate gift, see page 174 for a gift kit idea.

BENNY'S BACON

INGREDIENTS

3½ tablespoons fennel seeds

2 tablespoons whole black
   peppercorns

1½ tablespoons yellow mustard
   seeds

6 bay leaves

1 (10-pound) pork belly

2 teaspoons (10 grams) curing salt

1 cup packed light brown sugar

1 cup kosher salt

2 cups sweet pulverized wood chips,
   such as apple, cherry, alder, or oak

IMPLEMENTS

Medium Sauté Pan, Measuring
Cups and Spoons, Spice or Coffee
Grinder, Large Rimmed Baking
Sheet, Disposable Gloves, Cutting
Board, Slicing Knife, Stovetop
Smoker, Tongs, Meat Fork

Benjamin Bettinger is a star on the Portland, Oregon, food scene. He is the executive chef at Beaker & Flask, named Restaurant of the Year by *Willamette Week* in 2009, the restaurant's first year of operation. He also happens to make spectacular homemade bacon! We wanted to learn how to make bacon and thought how fun it would be to give homemade cured and smoked bacon as a gift. Ben generously shared his recipe. What sets Benny's bacon apart is the blend of spices, as most bacon recipes, whether commercial or homemade, do not include any spices other than black pepper in the curing rub. Pork bellies are available by special order from most butcher shops. They are usually about 10 pounds. This recipe will work without adjustment, give or take up to 1 pound. Use kitchen gloves to rub on the curing salt, as it can be highly irritating to the skin. Use pulverized wood chips sold for stovetop smoking, not the larger chips meant for outdoor grills.

Prep Time: 25 minutes | Curing Time: 5 days | Smoking Time: about 2¾ hours
| Makes four (2½-pound) slabs of bacon

1 In a medium, dry heavy skillet, preferably cast iron, toast the fennel seeds, peppercorns, mustard seeds, and bay leaves over medium-low heat. Swirl the spices in the pan until they release their aromas and take on a slightly darker color, 1 to 2 minutes. Immediately transfer the spice mixture to a spice or coffee grinder and grind to a powder.

2 Place the pork belly on a large rimmed baking sheet with the fat side down. Sprinkle the top (meat side) with about 40 percent of the curing salt, and then 40 percent of the spice powder. Wearing disposable gloves, rub the salt and spices into the meat. Next scatter about 40 percent of the brown sugar over the spices. Using muscle power, firmly press and rub the brown sugar into the flesh. Sprinkle about 40 percent of the kosher salt over the brown sugar and firmly press and rub the salt in, getting as much sugar and salt to absorb into the meat as possible. Flip the belly over so that the fat side is up and repeat this coating process with the remaining 60 percent of the curing salt, spice powder, brown sugar, and kosher salt.

3 Wrap the belly in several layers of plastic wrap; or place it in a food-safe plastic bag, squeeze out as much air as possible, and tie it closed. (This is how Ben does it.) Refrigerate the wrapped belly on the baking sheet with the fat side up for 5 days.

4 Slice the cured belly into 4 equal slabs, about 2½ pounds each.

5 Set up a stovetop smoker with the wood chips scattered on the bottom and the drip tray set on top. Wrap the wire rack in aluminum foil and set it over the drip tray. Working with one slab of belly at a time, place the belly on the foil-wrapped rack, close the lid of the smoker tightly, and turn the burner to medium-low. Smoke the belly for 20 minutes, then open the smoker lid, flip the belly over, and smoke it on the other side for an additional 20 minutes. At this point, check whether the belly is easily pierced with a meat fork. If it is, then remove it from the smoker. If not, flip the belly again and continue smoking until it is easily pierced. Remove the bacon from the smoker, wrap it tightly in plastic wrap, and refrigerate. Repeat this process with the 3 remaining slabs of belly.

STORING: *Refrigerate for up to 1 month or freeze for up to 1 year.*

GIFT CARD: This homemade spiced bacon was smoked on [give date] and can be enjoyed for up to 1 month, kept in the refrigerator, or 1 year if frozen. Slice it into ¼-inch-thick slices and pan-fry for breakfast. It is also delicious wrapped around a grilled filet mignon, and it makes the best BLT you'll ever taste!

GIFT-GIVING TIPS: Wrap each slab of bacon tightly in plastic wrap, and then wrap neatly with butcher paper. Tie each package with raffia or ribbon and attach a gift card. To turn this into a gift basket, consider including a dozen brown eggs fresh from the farmers' market and a breakfast-appropriate loaf of artisan bread. To make the gift more elaborate, include a butcher-block cutting board and a slicing knife, or see page 169 for a gift kit idea.

SALMON GRAVLAX

INGREDIENTS

½ cup coarse sea salt or kosher salt

½ cup granulated sugar

1 salmon fillet (3 to 4 pounds), skin on and scaled, pin bones removed

10 sprigs dill, coarsely chopped

¼ cup gin

IMPLEMENTS

Long (2-Inch-Deep) Glass or Ceramic Baking Dish, Small Bowl, Measuring Cups, Cutting Board, Chef's Knife, Smaller Baking Dish, Long Thin-Bladed Slicing Knife

One of the most delicate and least embellished salmon preparations is gravlax, a Scandinavian specialty in which the fish is cured by means of a salt and sugar rub. No cooking is involved. We like to think of this paper-thin sliced raw fish as one step beyond Japanese sashimi. Typically, gravlax is seasoned with fresh dill, a brandy such as Cognac, and spruce sprigs. Not everyone has a spruce tree growing in the yard, so we've decided to re-create that woodsy flavor by including gin in our recipe. The gin's mild juniper berry flavor is a lovely accent with the dill.

Prep Time: 20 minutes | Curing Time: 2 to 5 days | Makes one (3- to 4-pound) fillet of gravlax; once sliced, it can be portioned into three packages of six appetizer-size servings each

1 Select a 2-inch-deep glass or ceramic baking dish that fits the length of the fish as closely as possible. In a small bowl, combine the salt and sugar and spread half of this mixture on the bottom of the baking dish. Lay the salmon, skin side down, in the dish. Gently rub the remaining salt mixture over the flesh side of the fillet. Spread the dill over the fillet. Slowly drizzle the gin over the fish, being careful not to rinse off the salt cure.

2 Place a large sheet of plastic wrap directly on top of the fish. Select a slightly smaller baking dish, or some other large, flat object, to rest on top of the fish. Place something that weighs several pounds in the top of the dish. I use full beer bottles set on their sides.

3 Place the weighted salmon in the refrigerator for at least 2 days or up to 5 days. Turn the salmon over once a day, being sure to weight the salmon after each turn.

4 Once cured, skin the fillet, and then cut the fillet into ⅛-inch-thick crosswise slices. Arrange on a plate, wooden board, or in packages ready for gift giving. Cover tightly and refrigerate.

RECIPE CARD: CREATE A CARD TO PACKAGE WITH GIFT

GRAVLAX APPETIZER

Serve the salmon with buttered pumpernickel as an appetizer or first course along with thin slices of English cucumber. The salmon can be garnished with chopped chives, scallions, capers, minced shallots, or lemon zest. Drizzle the salmon with a little extra-virgin olive oil, if desired. Serves 6.

STORING: *Refrigerate, covered, for up to 1 week, or freeze for up to 3 months. (If freezing, wrap the gravlax completely in plastic wrap and then in a double layer of aluminum foil.)*

GIFT-GIVING TIPS: Thinly slice the salmon and arrange on a wooden board or plank, and then tightly seal with plastic wrap. Alternatively, portion the fillet into thirds, set each on a decorative fish plate, and then tightly seal with plastic wrap. Attach a recipe card. To turn this into a gift basket, consider including a loaf of pumpernickel bread or rye flatbreads, along with a jar of salt-cured capers and a tub of locally made cream cheese.

OLIVE OIL AND HERB–CURED ALBACORE TUNA

INGREDIENTS

6 cups olive oil

Freshly grated zest of 2 lemons

4 cloves garlic, smashed

4 sprigs thyme

2 sprigs rosemary

2 whole cloves

3 pounds fresh albacore tuna fillets, skin and dark blood spots removed

Kosher or sea salt

White vinegar

IMPLEMENTS

Eight (½-Pint) Glass Canning Jars, Pressure Canner and Rack (for Canned Tuna), Deep 12-Inch-Wide Sauté or Braising Pan, Measuring Cups and Spoons, Zester, Cutting Board, Chef's Knife, Instant-Read Thermometer, Slotted Spoon or Fish Spatula, Wide-Mouth Funnel, Small Ladle, Wooden Chopstick or Skewer, Canning Jar Lifter, Cooling Rack

After preserving our own tuna for the first time, we decided to do a side-by-side tasting of supermarket tuna and our home-cured version, and we were stunned at the difference. There was no comparison, and, honestly, the commercial canned tuna tasted like cat food! We've passed the point of no return and am now passionate about oil-poaching or canning our own tuna in season.

This recipe includes instructions for two different processes. The first involves poaching the tuna in an herb-infused olive oil and then packing the tuna, covered in the oil, in jars and refrigerating it for up to 2 weeks. You could call this "tuna confit"—a moist, delectably flaky style accented with olive oil, herb, lemon, and garlic flavor notes. Though this tuna has a relatively short shelf life, the reward is the ease of processing, and it makes the perfect gift when in season. The second method, equally delicious, requires a pressure canner to preserve the tuna. The advantage here is the shelf life: The tuna keeps on the pantry shelf for up to a year, which is a real boon for gift giving. Your landlocked friends will be rewarded with a delicious gift to savor any time or place that fresh-caught tuna is not available.

For canned tuna, you'll only need to make one-fourth of the infused oil. Follow the directions in Step 2, using a medium saucepan, 1½ cups of olive oil, the zest of half a lemon, 1 smashed clove garlic, 1 large sprig thyme, ½ sprig rosemary, and 1 whole clove.

Prep Time: 40 minutes | Processing Time for Poached Tuna: 30 minutes | Processing Time for Canned Tuna: 1 hour and 40 minutes | Makes about eight (½-pint) jars of poached or canned tuna

---

Huile

herb-cured
albacore tuna

1 Wash the jars, including the lids and screw bands, in hot, soapy water and dry thoroughly. Alternatively, run the jars through the regular cycle of your dishwasher; wash the lids and screw bands by hand. Sterilize the jars and lids. (See page 29.) If canning the tuna, have ready a pressure canner and rack that fits the bottom of the canner. (See page 5.)

2 Pour the oil into a wide sauté or braising pan. Add the lemon zest, garlic, thyme, rosemary, and cloves. Set the pan over low heat and heat the oil mixture to 160°F on an instant-read thermometer. Let the oil infuse for 15 minutes, adjusting the heat, if necessary, to maintain the temperature. Remove the oil from the heat and set aside.

3 For oil-poached tuna, proceed as follows: Cut the tuna fillets crosswise into 2-inch-thick slices. Lightly sprinkle the tuna with salt and rub the salt into the flesh. Arrange the slices in the oil, nestling them together and making sure they are completely submerged. Return the pan to low heat and bring the temperature of the oil back to 160°F. Maintaining that temperature, poach the tuna until cooked through, it flakes easily with a fork, and white pockets of fat appear on the surface of the fish, about 30 minutes. Using a slotted spoon or fish spatula, transfer the tuna to a cutting board. Set the oil aside to cool. Pack the tuna into the prepared jars, trimming the fillets to fit. Use the trimmings to fill the gaps in the jars, leaving 1 inch headspace. Using a wide-mouth funnel, ladle the oil over the tuna, making sure the tuna is completely covered with oil, leaving ½ inch headspace at the top. Remove any air bubbles by running a long wooden utensil, such as a chopstick or wooden skewer, between the jar and the tuna. Wipe the rims clean with a paper towel moistened with white vinegar. (This helps remove the oil from the rims.) Seal the jars and refrigerate.

4 For canned tuna, proceed as follows: Cut the tuna fillets crosswise into 1½-inch-thick slices. Pack the raw tuna into the prepared jars, trimming the fillets to fit. Use the trimmings to fill the gaps in the jars, leaving 1 inch headspace. Wipe the rims of the jars. Add ½ teaspoon of salt on top of the tuna in each jar. Using a wide-mouth funnel and filling one jar at a time, ladle the oil over the tuna, making sure the tuna is completely covered with oil, still leaving 1 inch headspace at the top. Remove any air bubbles by running a long wooden utensil, such as a chopstick or wooden skewer, between the jar and the tuna. Wipe the rims clean with a paper towel moistened with white vinegar. (This helps remove the oil from the rims.) Seal according to the manufacturer's directions. Process the jars in a pressure canner at 10 pounds of pressure for 1 hour and 40 minutes. (See page 5.) Turn off the heat and allow the pressure to drop to zero. Remove the gauge and then the top of the canner, tilting the lid away from you in case there is steam. Using a canning jar lifter, transfer the jars to a cooling rack, and allow the jars to rest until completely cool. Check the seals. It will be necessary to clean the jars before storing. Remove the screw bands and wash the jars and rims, taking care to protect the seals. Replace the screw bands and label.

STORING: *For the oil-poached tuna, refrigerate the jars for up to 2 weeks. For the canned tuna, store the jars in a cool, dark place for up to 1 year.*

GIFT CARD: This Olive Oil and Herb–Cured Albacore Tuna can be flaked to top a summertime niçoise salad; tossed with spaghetti, capers, oil-packed sun-dried tomatoes, and fresh herbs; broken into chunks in a cold Italian pasta salad; or made into the best tuna fish sandwich you've ever had! This tuna was preserved on [give date]. For oil-poached tuna, write: It can be enjoyed for up to 2 weeks, kept in the refrigerator. For canned tuna, write: Sealed, it will keep for up to 1 year. Once opened, keep refrigerated for up to 5 days.

GIFT-GIVING TIPS: Tie each jar with raffia or ribbon and attach a gift card. To turn this into a gift basket, consider including niçoise olives, salt-cured capers, eggs from the farmers' market, a crusty baguette, and a bottle of rosé wine.

DRIED PORCINI MUSHROOMS

INGREDIENTS
1½ pounds fresh porcini mushrooms

IMPLEMENTS
Mushroom Brush, Chef's Knife, Cutting Board, Food Dehydrator

Peck is a legendary food emporium in Milan that dates from 1883. It's a not-to-be-missed stop for foodies visiting Milan. When we last traveled to Italy, we shopped at Peck and brought home beautiful packages of dried porcini mushrooms to give as gifts. The perfectly sliced mushroom caps were arranged in overlapping rows nestled on top of soft, spaghetti-like strands of wood shavings and packed gorgeously in a shallow wooden crate sealed with cellophane. It was tied with a brown ribbon bow imprinted with "Peck" and its logo. With foraged porcini mushrooms available in season in the farmers' market, here's an opportunity to buy them fresh and dry your own. This is a precious gift to be given to your foodie friends—you'll be hugged!

Prep Time: 15 minutes | Drying Time: 8 to 12 hours | Makes 3 ounces dried porcini mushrooms, portioned into three (1-ounce) packages

1 Wipe any dirt from the mushrooms with a barely damp paper towel or use a mushroom brush. Trim the very base of the stems, only if necessary. Cut the mushrooms lengthwise, from the cap through the stem, into ¼-inch-thick slices.

2 Arrange the slices, without touching, on the mesh drying trays of a food dehydrator. Dry at 130°F until the slices feel dry and crisp with no signs of moisture on the inside, 8 to 12 hours.

RECIPE CARD: CREATE A CARD TO PACKAGE WITH GIFT

TAGLIATELLE WITH PORCINI MUSHROOMS, FIGS, AND SAGE

Soak the mushrooms in hot water to cover for 20 minutes. Bring a large pot of water to a boil for the pasta. Cook ½ pound tagliatelle until al dente. Meanwhile, in a large sauté pan, cook 3 slices of bacon cut into ½-inch pieces until crisp. Transfer the bacon to a plate lined with a paper towel. Drain all but 2 tablespoons of fat from the pan. Drain the mushrooms, pat dry, and coarsely chop; strain and reserve the mushroom soaking liquid. Over medium heat, sauté 2 thinly sliced shallots in the bacon fat until soft. Add the bacon, mushrooms, 5 quartered fresh figs, 6 thinly sliced sage leaves, ½ cup of the mushroom soaking liquid, salt, and pepper. Heat through. Drain the pasta and add to the sauce in the sauté pan. Toss with 3 tablespoons of extra-virgin olive oil. Divide among 4 warm pasta bowls. Shower with Parmigiano-Reggiano cheese. Serves 4.

STORING: *Store in a tightly covered tin or in cellophane bags. Do not store in plastic bags. Keep in a dark, cool, dry place for up to 1 year.*

GIFT-GIVING TIPS: Tie each cellophane bag or small clear gift box with raffia or ribbon and attach a recipe card. To turn this into a gift basket, consider including a pound of dried pasta, a bottle of extra-virgin olive oil, and a hunk of Parmigiano-Reggiano cheese. To make the gift a bit more elaborate, include a beautiful pasta bowl.

TO: Mom

I LOVE U

00536

005436

CHAPTER 8

BAKED *gifts*

Nothing says gifts from the heart more than gifts baked with love. Listen carefully and you can almost hear lips smack with sugar and spice and everything nice! But this is not just another *Adventures of Ozzie and Harriet* or *Brady Bunch* kitchen moment. Fast forward to the DIY era, and you can easily and creatively update your food gifts' repertoire with mouthwatering quick breads, biscotti, crackers, or skillet cornbread.

DOUBLE FUDGE BROWNIE POPS

INGREDIENTS

Vegetable oil cooking spray for
  preparing the pans

1 cup all-purpose flour

¾ cup plus 1 tablespoon sifted
  unsweetened cocoa powder

1½ teaspoons baking powder

¼ teaspoon kosher or sea salt

1 cup (2 sticks) unsalted butter,
  melted

1 cup granulated sugar

1 cup packed light brown sugar

3 large eggs

2 teaspoons pure vanilla extract

1 cup semisweet mini chocolate
  chips

6 to 8 ounces white chocolate

Red, green, or other seasonal
  sparkling sugars

Christmas-colored nonpareils or
  other seasonal holiday sprinkles

IMPLEMENTS

Wilton Silicone Brownie Pop Molds
(Preferably Two or Three Molds
Making Eight Pops Each), Large
Rimmed Baking Sheet, Measuring
Cups and Spoons, Medium Bowl,
Flour Sifter, Stand Mixer with
Paddle Attachment or Hand Mixer,
Rubber Spatula, 1½-Ounce (#30)
Ice-Cream Scoop or Small Spoon,
Cooling Rack, Microwave-Safe Small
Bowl, Soup Spoon, Twenty-Four
Lollipop/Brownie Pop Sticks

Is there anything more adorable than a brownie baked in a petite mold, decorated with icing and sprinkles, and secured on a lollipop stick? No way! Think of these as party favors, sweets for your colleagues at work, Christmastime stocking stuffers, or Halloween treats. The decorating fun is up to you: The white chocolate can be tinted using food coloring to match whatever holiday you are making these for—use pink for Valentine's Day, pastels for Easter, red and green for Christmas, or even orange for Halloween.

Prep Time: 30 minutes | Bake Time: 20 minutes per batch | Makes two dozen brownie pops

1   Position a rack in the center of the oven. Preheat the oven to 350°F. Spray the silicone molds with cooking spray to ensure the brownie pops won't stick. Set aside on a large rimmed baking sheet.

2   In a medium bowl, sift together the flour, cocoa, baking powder, and salt. Set aside.

3   In the bowl of a stand mixer fitted with the paddle attachment, beat together the butter and granulated and brown sugars on medium speed until blended, about 3 minutes. Add the eggs one at a time, beating well after each addition. Beat in the vanilla, and then stop and scrape down the sides of the bowl once with a rubber spatula.

4   With the mixer on low speed, add the sifted ingredients in 3 batches, beating after each addition until the flour disappears. Do not overmix. Using a rubber spatula, fold in the chocolate chips.

5 Using a small spoon or #30 ice-cream scoop, portion the batter into the molds, filling each cavity two-thirds full. Tap the molds on the counter to release any air bubbles. (Reserve the batter and bake the brownie pops in batches, if necessary.) Bake the brownie pops on the baking sheet until a toothpick inserted into the center comes out clean, about 20 minutes. Transfer the molds to a wire rack and let cool completely before releasing the brownie pops.

6 To decorate, set the brownie pops, flat side down, on a baking sheet lined with parchment or waxed paper.

7 Break the white chocolate into small chunks and place in a small microwave-safe bowl. Microwave on high for 2 minutes, stirring after 1 minute, until the chocolate is completely melted.

8 Using a soup spoon, drizzle the chocolate over the top of each brownie pop, allowing the chocolate to stream down the sides to form "legs." Before the chocolate sets, sprinkle the brownie pops with sparkling sugar and nonpareils. Carefully place a brownie pop stick in the center at the top, pushing until the stick is about three-quarters of the way into the brownie. If needed, add a few more sprinkles at the insertion point of the stick. Refrigerate until completely set, about 4 hours.

STORING: *Refrigerate uncovered for 4 hours. Wrap the brownie pops and keep refrigerated for up to 10 days.*

GIFT CARD: These Double Fudge Brownie Pops are a treat for the whole family or just the kids! Enjoy today, or keep refrigerated for up to [give number] days. (Calculate the date based on when you baked the brownie pops.)

GIFT-GIVING TIPS: Cut sheets of clear cellophane to form 8 by 10-inch rectangles. Cut ribbon into 13-inch lengths. Arrange a brownie pop in the center of a cellophane sheet. Bring up the sides and cinch closed at the top of the brownie, securing the cellophane with the ribbon and tying it around the lollipop stick. Tie a bow, and attach a gift card. Refrigerate until ready to give.

CRACKED PEPPER, DRIED CHERRY, AND CHOCOLATE CHUNK BISCOTTI

INGREDIENTS

2¼ cups all-purpose flour, plus
   more for dusting
1½ teaspoons baking powder
1 teaspoon ground cinnamon
½ teaspoon kosher or sea salt
⅓ cup unsalted butter, at room
   temperature
¾ cup granulated sugar
2 large eggs
1 teaspoon pure vanilla extract
1¼ cups dried cherries
¾ cup (3½-ounce bar) coarsely
   chopped dark bittersweet
   chocolate
1 teaspoon coarsely ground black
   pepper

IMPLEMENTS

Measuring Cups and Spoons,
Cutting Board, Chef's Knife, Pepper
Mill, Sifter, Medium Bowl, Stand
Mixer with Paddle Attachment or
Hand Mixer, Rubber Spatula, Two
Large Rimmed Nonstick Baking
Sheets, Serrated Knife, Spatula,
Cooling Rack

Making biscotti is easier than you think, and they are the perfect hostess gift at holiday time. Think about wrapping the biscotti in cellophane bags tied with ribbon and having multiple packages for co-workers or friends. In addition, they are ideal for a Christmastime cookie-swap party. There are three key ingredients that make these biscotti spectacular: chocolate, cherries, and black pepper. Use a deeply rich chocolate, such as Valrhona Le Noir Amer 71 percent cacao, and chop it into pea-size bits using a sharp chef's knife; be sure to include all the little shavings, as they melt deliciously into the dough. Look for dried Bing or tart cherries that are soft and plump, usually found in specialty markets. For big pepper flecks, a pepper mill with an adjustable grind mechanism or a mortar and pestle is the best way to grind whole peppercorns very coarsely.

Prep Time: 30 minutes | Bake Time: 55 minutes | Makes about three dozen biscotti

1 Position one rack in the center of the oven and another rack in the lower third of the oven. Preheat the oven to 325°F.

2 In a medium bowl, sift together the flour, baking powder, cinnamon, and salt. Set aside.

3 In the bowl of a stand mixer fitted with the paddle attachment, cream the butter and sugar until fluffy, about 3 minutes. Add the eggs one at a time, beating well after each addition. Mix in the vanilla.

4 With the mixer on low speed, add the sifted ingredients in 2 batches, beating after each addition until the flour disappears. Do not overmix. Using a rubber spatula, fold in the cherries, chocolate, and pepper.

5 Turn the mixture out onto a lightly floured work surface. The dough will be a bit sticky. Divide the dough in half. With lightly floured hands, roll each half into a log 1½ inches thick and about 15 inches long. Place both logs about 3 inches apart on a nonstick or parchment-lined baking sheet. Bake until lightly firm to the touch, about 25 minutes. Remove from the oven and let sit for 10 minutes.

6 Place one log on a cutting board. With a sharp serrated knife and using a sawing motion, carefully cut the log on a slight diagonal into ½-inch-thick slices. Place the slices on their sides on the baking sheet. Repeat with the second log, using an additional baking sheet to arrange the biscotti in a single layer. Bake until dried out and lightly golden, about 10 minutes. Turn each slice over and bake until lightly golden, 10 minutes longer. Transfer to wire racks to cool completely.

STORING: *Layer the biscotti in an airtight container between sheets of waxed paper. Store at room temperature for up to 1 week.*

GIFT CARD: These home-baked Cracked Pepper, Dried Cherry, and Chocolate Chunk Biscotti were made on [give date] and can be enjoyed for up to 1 week. They are delectable dunked in espresso or brewed coffee and downright decadent served, as the Italians do, after dinner with *vin santo* or grappa.

GIFT-GIVING TIPS: Wrap the biscotti in cellophane bags tied with a ribbon, or layer in attractive tins or laminated gift boxes lined with decorative waxed paper. Attach a gift card. To turn this into a gift basket, consider including gourmet coffee and fun, seasonal mugs. Alternatively, include a bottle of *vin santo* or a digestif, such as grappa, both of which are traditional for dunking biscotti.

MINI APRICOT AND CRYSTALLIZED GINGER QUICK BREADS

INGREDIENTS

Vegetable oil cooking spray for
   preparing the pans

3½ cups all-purpose flour

4 teaspoons baking powder

1 teaspoon kosher or sea salt

½ teaspoon baking soda

½ teaspoon ground cinnamon

⅛ teaspoon freshly grated nutmeg

⅔ cup (1 stick plus 3 tablespoons)
   unsalted butter, at room
   temperature

1⅓ cups granulated sugar

4 large eggs, at room temperature

2 cups mashed ripe bananas (about
   4 bananas)

1⅓ cups finely chopped dried
   apricots, tossed with 1 tablespoon
   of flour to separate

¾ cup chopped hazelnuts or
   walnuts, toasted (see Note)

½ cup diced crystallized ginger

IMPLEMENTS

Five (6 by 2½-Inch) Italian-Made
Heavy Waxed Paper Loaf Pans, Large
Rimmed Baking Sheet, Measuring
Cups and Spoons, Large Bowl, Flour
Sifter, Stand Mixer with Paddle
Attachment or Hand Mixer, Rubber
Spatula, Cooling Rack

This is a favorite quick bread, and it makes a delectable hostess gift. A loaf quickly disappears if sliced and set out for breakfast on a lazy weekend. It is best when toasted and smeared with a little butter. The tiny pockets of tender, sweet apricot and brightly flavored ginger mingle on the palate while the warm banana bread speckled with toasted walnuts brings delight to the morning meal. This recipe yields five miniature loaves or two standard loaves. For gift giving, you can buy lovely, Italian-made paper baking pans that come in mini loaf pan sizes. Bake right in these disposable, heavy waxed paper pans that are brown-toned with a decorative gold pattern. Leave the loaves in the pans and wrap with clear cellophane and a bright bow.

Prep Time: 45 minutes | Bake Time: 25 minutes | Makes five (6 by 2½-inch) miniature loaves or two (9 by 5-inch) standard loaves

1 Position a rack in the center of the oven. Preheat the oven to 350°F. Spray the bottom and sides of the loaf pans with cooking spray. Set aside on a large rimmed baking sheet.

2 In a large bowl, sift together the flour, baking powder, salt, baking soda, cinnamon, and nutmeg. Set aside.

3 In the bowl of a stand mixer fitted with the paddle attachment, cream together the butter and sugar on medium speed until fluffy, about 3 minutes. Add the eggs one at a time, beating well after each addition. Beat in the bananas, stopping and scraping down the sides of the bowl once with a rubber spatula.

4 With the mixer on low speed, add the sifted ingredients in 3 batches, beating after each addition until the flour disappears. Do not overmix. Using a rubber spatula, fold in the apricots, nuts, and ginger.

5 Divide the batter between the prepared pans. Bake the mini loaves on the baking sheet for 15 minutes, or 35 minutes if you're using two larger loaf pans. Rotate the pan 180 degrees and continue to bake until nicely browned, puffed at the center, and a toothpick inserted in the center comes out clean, about 10 minutes longer for either size loaf pans. Transfer the loaves to a wire rack and let cool in the pans.

Note: Spread the chopped nuts in a single layer on a rimmed baking sheet and bake on the center rack in a preheated 350°F oven until lightly browned and fragrant, about 5 minutes. (Watch carefully so they brown but don't burn!) Transfer to a plate to cool.

STORING: *The bread will keep for up to 5 days. Wrap the breads tightly with plastic wrap or place in sealable plastic bags with all the air removed. The bread can be frozen for up to 1 month.*

GIFT CARD: This Apricot and Crystallized Ginger Quick Bread is a fabulous breakfast treat for the busy host! Slice the bread, toast it, and smear it with a little softened butter.

GIFT-GIVING TIPS: Cut large rectangles of clear cellophane and wrap the loaves, tying them at the top with raffia or ribbon. Attach a gift card. To turn this into a gift basket, consider including a package of the mini loaf pans, dried apricots, nuts, and crystallized ginger; tuck in a recipe card with the recipe for the bread. For a more elaborate gift, see page 169 for a gift kit idea.

JALAPEÑO AND CHEDDAR SKILLET CORNBREAD WITH HONEY BUTTER

INGREDIENTS

1¾ cups medium-grind yellow
cornmeal

1¼ cups all-purpose flour

⅓ cup granulated sugar

1 tablespoon baking powder

2 teaspoons kosher or sea salt

1¾ cups buttermilk

3 large eggs, beaten

1 (15-ounce) can creamed corn

½ cup canned diced jalapeños,
drained

½ cup (2 ounces) shredded sharp
cheddar cheese

6 tablespoons (¾ stick) unsalted
butter, melted

1 tablespoon bacon drippings or
melted butter, for greasing pan

Honey Butter

1½ cups (3 sticks) unsalted butter,
at room temperature

½ cup honey

IMPLEMENTS

Large and Medium Bowls, Measuring
Cups and Spoons, Can Opener, Box
Grater, Whisk, Rubber Spatula,
Three (6½-Inch) Seasoned Cast-Iron
Skillets, Ladle, Wire Rack, Food
Processor, Waxed Paper, Scissors,
Clear Cellophane

This is a gift to bake and give immediately. Though the honey butter stays fresh in the refrigerator for up to a month, the cornbread is best when eaten within a day or two of being made, so plan your gift giving accordingly. For friends, family, or co-workers who enjoy cooking but might not have a kitchen full of equipment, they'll receive a home-baked gift and a skillet to boot. The honey butter looks adorable and country-chic when formed into a log, rolled in waxed paper, and tied with raffia. Giving the honey butter packed into a butter bell is an alternative way to make the gift more elaborate.

Prep Time: 25 minutes | Bake Time: 30 to 35 minutes | Makes three (6½-inch) skillet cornbreads and three logs honey butter

1 To make the cornbread, position one rack in the center of the oven. Preheat the oven to 375°F.

2 In a large bowl, combine the cornmeal, flour, sugar, baking powder, and salt. In a medium bowl, combine the buttermilk and eggs. Add the buttermilk mixture to the dry ingredients, stirring just to blend. Fold in the creamed corn, jalapeños, and cheese. Stir in the melted butter.

3 Coat the cast-iron skillets with the bacon drippings. Place the greased pans in the oven until hot, 3 to 5 minutes. Remove from the oven and immediately ladle the batter into the heated pans, dividing it evenly. Bake until the cornbread is golden brown and a toothpick inserted in the center comes out clean, about 30 minutes. Let cool in the pans on a wire rack. Wrap tightly once the cornbread is completely cool.

4 To make the honey butter, place the butter and honey in a food processor fitted with the metal blade and process until completely blended and smooth, stopping the machine once or twice to scrape down the sides of the bowl. Cut three (8-inch-wide) sheets of waxed paper. Using a rubber spatula and table knife, transfer one-third of the honey butter to the center of each sheet of waxed paper. Form a log about 1½ inches in diameter and 4 inches long. Starting at the bottom edge, roll up the waxed paper, covering the butter and rolling it on the counter to form a smooth log. Twist the ends, tie with raffia or ribbon, and trim with scissors. Refrigerate the honey butter logs.

STORING: *Keep the cornbread in the pans. Cut 3 large sheets of clear cellophane and three 14-inch lengths of ribbon or raffia. Place a skillet in the center of a cellophane sheet and bring up the edges to tightly wrap the skillet and the bread. Tie securely with ribbon or raffia. Repeat with the remaining skillets of cornbread. Store at room temperature for up to 1 day. The honey butter will keep in the refrigerator for up to 1 month.*

GIFT CARD: This home-baked Jalapeño and Cheddar Skillet Cornbread was made on [give date] and should be eaten right away. Cut the cornbread into wedges and warm it before serving. The Honey Butter can be refrigerated and enjoyed for up to 1 month. Soften the butter at room temperature before serving.

GIFT-GIVING TIPS: Since the cornbread is being given in a cast-iron skillet, consider writing the recipe on a fun gift card and attaching it so that the recipient can make the cornbread again. To make the gift more elaborate, pack the honey butter in a butter bell rather than forming it into a log and wrapping it in waxed paper. Arrange the wrapped skillet and butter bell in a decorative, towel-lined basket. See page 169 for a gift kit idea.

COCONUT GRANOLA CRUNCH

INGREDIENTS

⅔ cup packed light brown sugar

½ cup canola oil

½ cup honey

2 teaspoons pure vanilla extract

2 teaspoons kosher or sea salt

2 teaspoons ground cinnamon

½ teaspoon freshly ground nutmeg

4 cups rolled oats

1 cup whole unsalted almonds

1 cup whole skinned hazelnuts

½ cup ground flax seeds

2 cups large-flake unsweetened coconut

2 cups dried fruit, either golden raisins, dried cherries, sweetened cranberries, chopped dates, apricots, or a favorite combination

IMPLEMENTS

Measuring Cups and Spoons, Large Bowl, Silicone Spatula, Two Large Nonstick Rimmed Baking Sheets, Two Large Cooling Racks

You'll be snacking on this before it ever gets scooped from the baking sheets and packed into the gift bags—it is so addictively good! It's better than any store-bought granola we've ever tasted. It's a deliciously healthy gift to give, packed with plant-derived omega-3 fatty acids from the canola oil and ground flax seeds, protein-charged with almonds and hazelnuts, and nutrient-rich with the addition of dried fruit. Customize the granola by substituting different nuts, such as walnuts and cashews, and select your own assortment of dried fruit. If giving this granola at Christmastime, the addition of dried cherries or sweetened cranberries makes it look seasonal and festive.

Prep Time: 15 minutes | Bake Time: 40 minutes | Makes 12 cups granola, portioned into four (3-cup) packages

1 Position one rack in the center of the oven and another rack in the lower third of the oven. Preheat the oven to 325°F.

2 In a large bowl, combine the sugar, oil, honey, vanilla extract, salt, cinnamon, and nutmeg. Stir until combined; however, the oil will not blend into the paste and that's okay. Add the oats to the mixture and use your hands to massage the ingredients together. Gently crush some of the oats with your fingers.

3 Divide the oat mixture between 2 large nonstick rimmed baking sheets and spread the small clumps of oats evenly with a silicon spatula. Bake for 15 minutes, then remove the pans from the oven. Sprinkle ½ cup of almonds over each pan of oats and stir to combine. Return the pans to the oven, switching the pans between the racks, and bake for 5 minutes more.

4 Remove the pans from the oven and divide the hazelnuts and flax seeds equally between the pans, stir. Return the pans to the oven, rotating them between the racks, and bake for 10 minutes longer.

5 Remove the pans from the oven and divide the coconut evenly between the pans, stirring to mix. Return the pans to the oven, switching the pans one last time, and continue to bake until the coconut is a light golden brown, 5 to 10 minutes longer.

6 Remove the granola from the oven, set on wire racks, and let cool on the pans. (Don't worry if the granola doesn't feel crisp; it will dry out and crisp up as it cools.) Once cool, stir in the dried fruit, dividing evenly between the pans.

STORING: *Store the granola at room temperature in tightly sealed glass jars or cellophane bags for up to 1 month.*

GIFT CARD: This homemade Coconut Granola Crunch was made on [give date] and can be enjoyed for up to 1 month, stored at room temperature. Enjoy it for breakfast with cold milk, layered with yogurt and fresh fruit for a breakfast parfait, or sprinkled over frozen yogurt for a healthy dessert.

GIFT-GIVING TIPS: Tie each glass jar or cellophane bag with raffia or ribbon and attach a gift card.

INGREDIENTS

3 tablespoons unsalted butter, melted

1½ cups all-purpose flour

2 tablespoons unsweetened cocoa powder

2 teaspoons ground cinnamon

1 teaspoon ground coriander

1 teaspoon ground ginger

½ teaspoon freshly grated nutmeg

½ teaspoon coarsely ground black pepper

½ teaspoon kosher or sea salt

¼ teaspoon ground cloves

2 cups whole unsalted almonds, toasted

2½ cups hazelnuts, toasted and skinned

2 cups dried apricots, cut into ¼-inch dice

2 cups dried Mission figs, cut into ¼-inch dice

1 cup dried cherries

1 cup store-bought candied orange peel, cut into ¼-inch dice

1½ cups granulated sugar

1½ cups honey

½ cup water

Confectioners' sugar, for dusting

IMPLEMENTS

Two (8 by 2-Inch) Springform Pans, Parchment Paper, Scissors, Measuring Cups and Spoons, Cutting Board, Chef's Knife, Large and Small Bowls, Pepper Mill, Rubber Spatula, 2-Quart Saucepan, Candy Thermometer, Silicone Spatula, Large Rimmed Baking Sheet, Cooling Rack

Panforte is a cross between a cake and a confection—a heavenly, dense, sumptuous dessert loaded with nuts, dried fruit, candied fruit, and spices. It is a popular and classic Christmastime treat from Siena, Italy, served as a snack or with a glass of *vin santo* for a holiday dessert. As suggested in the Gift-Giving Tips, a thin wedge of panforte served with a slice of cheese makes a delightful pairing for a cheese course following Christmas dinner.

Prep Time: 45 minutes | Bake Time: 60 to 70 minutes | Makes two (8-inch) cakes

1 Position one rack in the center of the oven. Preheat the oven to 300°F. Using the bottom of the pan as your measure, trace two 8-inch circles on the parchment and cut them out. Generously butter the bottom and sides of the pans, press a parchment paper round on the bottom of each pan, and butter the parchment. Set aside.

2 In a large bowl, mix together the flour, cocoa powder, cinnamon, coriander, ginger, nutmeg, pepper, salt, and cloves. Add the nuts, fruits, and candied orange peel, stirring to coat them evenly with the dry ingredients. Set aside.

3 In a 2-quart saucepan, combine the sugar, honey, and water. Place over medium heat and cook, stirring frequently, to dissolve the sugar, 3 to 5 minutes. When the mixture comes to a boil, decrease the heat to low, attach a candy thermometer to the side of the pan, and continue to boil, without stirring, until it reaches soft-ball stage (240°F on a candy thermometer), about 5 minutes longer. (It is important to not overcook the sugar mixture and take it past soft-ball stage; it will be sticky and too hard to spread.)

4 Immediately remove the sugar mixture from the heat and pour it over the nut and fruit mixture. Stir until well combined; it will be sticky and dense. Divide the mixture between the prepared pans, spreading it evenly to the edges and smoothing the top with a rubber spatula. Set the pans on a large rimmed baking sheet.

5 Bake the cakes until puffed and dark golden brown, about 1 hour. Transfer to wire racks and cool completely. When the cakes have cooled, run a damp table knife around the edges before releasing the latch on the springform pans. Remove the sides of each pan, slide the cakes off the bottom of the pans, and carefully remove the parchment. Dust the tops generously with confectioners' sugar.

6 For gift giving, the panforte can be given as a whole cake, cut into quarters, or even cut into thick wedges. Wrap tightly with plastic wrap or clear cellophane.

STORING: *Tightly wrap the panforte in plastic wrap or clear cellophane and store at room temperature for up to 1 month.*

GIFT CARD: This Panforte was made on [give date] and can be enjoyed for up to 1 month, tightly covered and stored at room temperature. Do as the Italians do and serve a thin wedge of panforte with cheese and a glass of *vin santo.*

GIFT-GIVING TIPS: Depending on whether you are giving an entire cake, quarter portions, or a thick wedge, the panforte can be wrapped and given in a laminated gift box, wrapped and set on a decorative plate, or double wrapped with cellophane first and then white butcher paper and butcher's twine, as it might be sold in Italy. To turn this into a gift basket, consider including a wedge of cheese, such as Morbier, and a bottle of *vin santo;* or see page 166 for a gift kit idea.

BISCOTTI CHRISTMAS TREE

INGREDIENTS

4½ cups all-purpose flour, plus more
   for dusting

4 teaspoons baking powder

½ teaspoon baking soda

1½ teaspoons ground cinnamon

1 teaspoon ground coriander

1 teaspoon kosher or sea salt

½ teaspoon ground cloves

¾ cup (1½ sticks) unsalted butter, at
   room temperature

1 cup granulated sugar

4 large eggs

2 tablespoons grated orange zest

2 teaspoons pure vanilla extract

1½ cups unsalted shelled pistachios

1 cup sweetened dried cranberries

Marmalade Icing

4 cups (1 pound) confectioners'
   sugar, plus more for dusting

¾ cup orange marmalade

2 tablespoons orange juice or orange-
   flavored liqueur, such as Cointreau

IMPLEMENTS

Three Sturdy (15 by 12-Inch) Baking
Sheets, Parchment Paper, Measuring
Cups and Spoons, Sifter, Large Bowl,
Zester, Stand Mixer with Paddle
Attachment or Hand Mixer, Rubber
Spatula, Kitchen Scale (optional),
Long Plastic Ruler, Cutting Board,
Long Serrated Knife, Spatula, Cooling
Rack, Chef's Knife, Small Microwave-
Safe Bowl, Pastry Bag and ¼-Inch
Plain Tip, Large Flat Platter

Here's a spectacular dessert and centerpiece all in one! This recipe was inspired by a Christmastime article that appeared in *Sunset* magazine in 1992. Think of giving this biscotti tree to a friend or family member who is hosting a holiday brunch, open house, or family dinner. It would certainly wow your co-workers to present this at a holiday office party. Decorate the tree on a platter you plan to give, or specify that the platter is "on loan." Alternatively, you could build the biscotti tree on a decorative disposable platter or even on a large Lucite square. Explain that the tree is meant to be eaten, and encourage guests to gently remove individual cookies starting from the top of the tree—after all, this isn't a game of Jenga!

Prep Time: 1½ hours | Bake Time: 40 minutes | Assembly Time: 45 minutes | Makes one large biscotti tree with about four dozen cookies of varying length

1 Have ready 3 sturdy 15 by 12-inch baking sheets lined with parchment paper.

2 In a large bowl, sift together the flour, baking powder, baking soda, cinnamon, coriander, salt, and cloves. Set aside.

3 In the bowl of a stand mixer fitted with the paddle attachment, cream the butter and sugar until fluffy, about 3 minutes. Add the eggs one at a time, beating well after each addition. Mix in the orange zest and vanilla.

4 With the mixer on low speed, add the sifted ingredients in 3 batches, beating after each addition until the flour disappears. Do not overmix. Using a rubber spatula, fold in the nuts and cranberries.

5 Turn the mixture out onto lightly floured work surface. The dough will be a bit sticky. Divide
   the dough into 3 equal portions. (It would be ideal if you had a scale to weigh the portions.
   Each portion weighs 18 ounces.) With lightly floured hands, and working with one portion at a
   time, place the dough in the center of the parchment-lined pan. Pat each piece into an evenly
   thick flat-topped triangle that measures 9 inches across the base, 2 inches across the top, and
   12 inches on the sides. Use a long plastic ruler to measure the sides and form clean, straight
   edges by pressing the ruler alongside the dough. Repeat with the remaining portions of dough.
   As you finish forming the triangles, place them in the refrigerator to chill for 30 minutes.

6 While the dough is resting, position one rack in the center of the oven and another rack in the
   lower third of the oven. Preheat the oven to 350°F. (If you happen to have two ovens or a large
   oven with 3 oven racks, you can bake all the biscotti at once. Otherwise, you'll need to bake
   the biscotti in batches.)

7 Bake the biscotti until just beginning to turn light brown at the edges, 15 to 20 minutes. Switch
   the pans between the racks at the midpoint of baking so that they bake evenly. Remove from
   the oven and cool for 5 minutes.

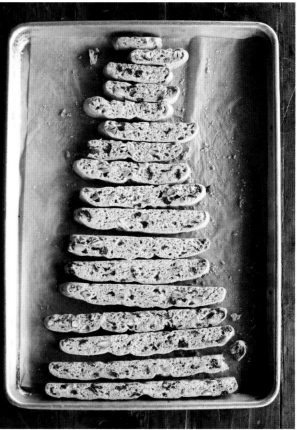

8   Working with one partially baked biscotti triangle at a time, carefully transfer the parchment sheet to a large cutting board. Using a long serrated knife and a ruler, begin at the base of the triangle and position the ruler parallel to the base. Using a sawing motion, precisely measure and cut the triangle into ⅝-inch-wide slices, working your way up to the top. Repeat to cut the remaining baked triangles.

9   Place the slices on their sides on the unlined baking sheets. Bake until dried out and lightly golden, about 10 minutes. Turn each slice over and bake until lightly golden, about 10 minutes longer. Transfer to wire racks to cool completely. (The biscotti can be made 1 to 2 days in advance. Store in a covered container at room temperature.)

10 To assemble the biscotti tree, first make the marmalade icing. Sift the confectioners' sugar into the bowl of a stand mixer fitted with the paddle attachment or into a large bowl and use a hand mixer. Pick out and finely mince the pieces of orange peel from the marmalade. Add the minced peel back into the marmalade and then warm it in a microwave to liquefy it, about 30 seconds. Add the marmalade and orange juice to the sifted sugar and beat for 5 minutes. The icing will be silky and glistening, and all the sugar will be absorbed. Transfer to a pastry bag fitted with a ¼-inch plain tip. Set aside.

11 Have ready a large flat platter. Select the 3 longest cookies. Pipe the icing on one of the cut sides of each cookie. Lay, icing side down, on the platter with the tips touching to form a large triangle. Pipe a long thick line of icing along the length of each cookie. Select the next 3 longest cookies, and create a Star of David by arranging them in a triangle shape, with tips touching, on top of the base triangle. Pipe a long thick line of icing along the length of each cookie. Continue to build the tree by repeating this process of layering the cookies and icing each layer, selecting the next longest cookies for each layer, finishing with the small 2-inch cookies for the top. Use extra icing to drip "icicles" at the edges or along the sides. Dust the tree with confectioners' sugar "snow." Decorate the platter with holly sprigs and faux red berry clusters, if desired.

STORING: *The Biscotti Christmas Tree can be assembled and stored, uncovered, in a cool, dry spot for up to 3 days.*

GIFT CARD: This Biscotti Christmas Tree is delightful to look at but is also meant to be eaten! Encourage your guests to sample a cookie by gently lifting a cookie from the top of the tree, carefully removing them layer by layer.

GIFT-GIVING TIPS: To transport the tree, set the platter in a large, shallow, sturdy box and cover loosely with aluminum foil. Tuck in a gift card. (Carry it carefully and drive slowly!)

RUSTIC ROSEMARY-PARMESAN CRACKERS

INGREDIENTS

2¼ cups (10 ounces) tipo "00" flour or unbleached all-purpose flour, plus more for dusting (see page 7)

1½ tablespoons finely minced fresh rosemary

½ teaspoon kosher or sea salt

¼ teaspoon granulated sugar

¾ cup water

2 tablespoons extra-virgin olive oil, plus more for brushing pans

6 tablespoons freshly grated Parmesan cheese, preferably Parmigiano-Reggiano

IMPLEMENTS

Measuring Cups and Spoons, Stand Mixer with Dough Hook, Pastry Brush, Two Large Rimmed Nonstick Baking Sheets, Rolling Pin, Bench Scraper, Ruler, Fluted Pastry Cutter, Spatula, Cooling Rack

These thin, crisp cracker strips make the perfect hostess gift. Not only do they look adorable with their golden brown color and fluted edges, but their savory flavor makes for irresistible nibbles, whether served on their own or dipped into a soft olive tapenade.

Prep Time: 45 minutes | Rest Time: 30 minutes | Bake Time: about 30 minutes | Makes four dozen crackers

1 In the bowl of a stand mixer fitted with the dough hook, combine the flour, rosemary, salt, and sugar. Pour the water over the top and begin mixing on low speed until the ingredients come together. Increase to medium speed and knead the dough for 5 minutes, stopping the mixer once or twice if the dough crawls up the dough hook. Remove the dough and wrap it tightly in plastic wrap. Set aside at room temperature for 30 minutes. This allows the gluten to relax.

2 While the dough is resting, position one rack in the center of the oven. Preheat the oven to 375°F. Generously brush 2 large rimmed baking sheets with olive oil. Set aside.

3 To make the crackers, divide the dough in half. Rewrap one portion so it doesn't dry out. Dust a work surface generously with flour. Dust the top of the dough with flour. With a rolling pin, roll out the dough into a large thin 24 by 8-inch rectangle. Brush the surface with 1 tablespoon of the olive oil and evenly sprinkle 3 tablespoons of the Parmesan over the top. Using a ruler and fluted pastry cutter, cut the dough crosswise into 8 by 1-inch strips. Carefully transfer the dough strips to the prepared baking sheets, arranging them 1 inch apart.

4   For even browning, it is important to bake only one pan of crackers at a time. Bake the crackers until they are golden with bubbled spots of brown on the bottom and top, 8 to 10 minutes. Do not let the ends overbake. Crackers positioned at the ends of the pan tend to brown more quickly, so transfer those to wire racks as needed and continue baking the remaining crackers until golden and crisp. Transfer to wire racks to cool.

5   Repeat with the remaining dough. Wipe the baking sheets with paper towels to remove any bits of dough and cheese. Generously brush the pans again with olive oil and bake as directed above. Let the crackers cool completely.

STORING: *Layer the crackers in an airtight container between sheets of waxed paper. Do not store in plastic bags. Store at room temperature for up to 1 month.*

GIFT CARD: Enjoy these Rustic Rosemary-Parmesan Crackers today, or keep tightly sealed for up to [give number] weeks. (Calculate the date based on when you baked the crackers.) If desired, the crackers can be refreshed in a 350°F oven for 5 minutes. As a nibble with a glass of wine, they are delectable on their own, but they also can be used as a dipper for soft spreads or dips or served alongside a wedge of cheese.

GIFT-GIVING TIPS: Wrap the crackers in long cellophane bags tied with a ribbon or raffia and attach a gift card. To turn this into a gift basket, consider including a savory spread, such as an herbed goat cheese or olive tapenade, along with a bottle of wine. For a more elaborate gift, see page 166 for a gift kit idea.

CINNAMON-COATED GRAHAM CRACKERS

INGREDIENTS

1½ cups graham flour, plus more for
    dusting

¾ cup all-purpose flour

¾ teaspoon kosher or sea salt

½ teaspoon baking soda

½ teaspoon ground cinnamon

4 tablespoons (½ stick) unsalted
    butter, at room temperature

⅓ cup packed light brown sugar

1 large egg, beaten

¼ cup honey

2 teaspoons pure vanilla extract

Cinnamon-Sugar Topping

¼ cup turbinado sugar

1½ teaspoons ground cinnamon

IMPLEMENTS

Measuring Cups and Spoons,
Medium Bowl, Flour Sifter, Stand
Mixer with Paddle Attachment or
Hand Mixer, Rubber Spatula, Small
Bowl, Rolling Pin, Ruler, Dinner
Knife, Fluted Pastry Cutter or Paring
Knife, Toothpick or Wooden Skewer,
Two Large Rimmed Baking Sheets,
Parchment Paper or Nonstick Baking
Liners, Cooling Rack

These are beyond adorable, more spectacular than any graham cracker you have ever tasted from a box, and such an unexpected gift. We made up generous gift bags but had to gift some back to the cook for snacking—we just couldn't part with them. Give these to friends and family who have children, as the recipe card tells you how to turn these crackers into an ooey-gooey delectable treat of s'mores. And you don't need a campfire to make them.

Prep Time: 30 minutes | Bake Time: 14 minutes | Makes forty (2-inch square) graham crackers

1 In a large bowl, sift together the graham flour, all-purpose flour, salt, baking soda, and cinnamon. Set aside.

2 In the bowl of a stand mixer fitted with the paddle attachment, beat together the butter, sugar, and egg on medium-high speed until smooth and creamy, about 3 minutes. Add the honey and vanilla and beat until smooth, stopping and scraping down the sides of the bowl once with a rubber spatula.

3 With the mixer on low speed, add the sifted ingredients in 2 batches, beating after each addition until the flour disappears. Do not overmix. The dough should hold together and feel manageable for rolling.

4 Press the dough into a flat disk, cover with plastic wrap, and refrigerate for 30 minutes.

5 While the dough is chilling, make the cinnamon-sugar topping. In a small bowl, combine the turbinado sugar and cinnamon. Set aside.

6   Position one rack in the center of the oven and another rack in the lower third of the oven. Preheat the oven to 350°F. Line 2 rimmed baking sheets with parchment paper or nonstick baking liners, or use nonstick baking sheets.

7   Transfer the dough to a work surface liberally dusted with graham flour. Dust the top of the dough with graham flour. Using a lightly floured rolling pin, roll out the dough into an ⅛-inch-thick rectangle. Use a ruler to measure and a dinner knife to lightly mark 2-inch squares. Using a fluted pastry cutter or paring knife, cut out the squares and transfer to the prepared baking sheets, spacing the crackers 1 inch apart. Place the pan of crackers in the refrigerator while you roll the remaining crackers. Gather up the dough scraps, lightly dust with graham flour, reroll the dough, and cut out crackers until all the dough is used. Using the blunt side of a toothpick or wooden skewer, prick each cracker to form a 3 by 3 grid of evenly spaced holes (9 holes total). Using your fingers, sprinkle each cracker generously with the cinnamon-sugar topping.

8   Bake the crackers until firm and nicely browned, about 14 minutes. Switch the pans between the racks at the midpoint of baking if the crackers appear to be baking unevenly. Transfer to wire racks and cool completely.

RECIPE CARD: CREATE A CARD TO PACKAGE WITH GIFT

S'MORES WITHOUT A CAMPFIRE

Position a rack in the upper third of the oven. Preheat the oven to 400°F. Place 4 graham crackers on a rimmed baking sheet. Break the chocolate bars into sections a little smaller than the graham crackers. Place a section of chocolate on top of each cracker. Top the chocolate with 2 marshmallows. Bake until the marshmallows puff and are lightly toasted and the chocolate is warm and softened, 5 to 7 minutes. Transfer to dessert plates. Drizzle a little warm chocolate sauce over the top and eat while hot! Serves 4.

STORING: *Layer the graham crackers in an airtight container between sheets of waxed paper. Store at room temperature for up to 3 weeks.*

GIFT-GIVING TIPS: Wrap the crackers in attractive tins or laminated gift boxes lined with decorative waxed paper. To turn this into a gift basket, consider including marshmallows, 2 bars of semisweet or dark chocolate, a jar of rich-tasting chocolate sauce, and the following recipe for s'mores.

CHAPTER 9

CONFECTIONS
& CHOCOLATE *gifts*

These confections and chocolates are the stuff that dreams are made of. In fact, your family and friends might even ask you to pinch them when they unwrap these scrumptious, eye- and palate-pleasing homemade gifts. That—and the fun you had in the kitchen making them—will be ample reward for your investment of time and talent in creating your own. Wrap up puffy Toasted Coconut Marshmallows and Roasted White Chocolate–Dipped Apples as family treats, or deliver Blackberry-Merlot Jellies and divine chocolate bark as after-dinner delights.

BLACKBERRY-MERLOT JELLIES

INGREDIENTS

1 pint (¾ pound) fresh blackberries

¾ cup merlot

2¼ cups granulated sugar

1½ tablespoons freshly squeezed
lemon juice

1 (1½-inch-long) cinnamon stick

1 tablespoon raspberry liqueur, such
as Chambord

½ teaspoon pure vanilla extract

Pinch of kosher or sea salt

2 (3-ounce) pouches liquid pectin
(see page 13)

Superfine sugar, for coating

IMPLEMENTS

Medium Saucepan, Measuring
Cup and Spoons, Juicer, Silicone
Spatula, Parchment Paper, 12 by
8 by 1-Inch Jellyroll Pan, Fine-
Mesh Strainer, Medium Bowl, Deep
4-Quart Saucepan, Scissors, Glass
Measuring Cup, Plate, Cutting
Board, Ruler, Long Thin-Bladed
Sharp Knife

Making these jellies involves a simple two-step process:
First, an infusion is made by steeping plump blackberries
fresh from the farmers' market in a spiced wine mixture;
then the infusion is used to make these amazing, jewel-
toned jellies like those you see on petit four plates at
elegant French restaurants. These are absolutely precious
and beyond delicious—lightly crusted in shimmering
superfine sugar, the flavor lingers in your mouth for what
seems like eternity.

Prep Time: 20 minutes | Cook Time: 40 minutes | Set Time: 3 hours | Makes
about eighty-six (1-inch-square) jellies

1 In a medium saucepan, combine the berries, merlot, ¼ cup of
the granulated sugar, lemon juice, and cinnamon stick. Bring
the mixture to a boil over medium-high heat, stirring to dissolve
the sugar. Decrease to a simmer and cook, uncovered, for 10
minutes. Remove from the heat, cover the pan with plastic
wrap, and allow the flavors to infuse for 30 minutes.

2 Meanwhile, cut a rectangle of parchment paper to fit the bottom of a 12 by 8 by 1-inch jellyroll pan. Set aside.

3 Set a fine-mesh strainer over a medium bowl. Strain the berry
mixture, pressing on the solids with a silicone spatula to extract
all the liquid. (Do not purée the mixture and then extract the
seeds or the sauce will turn cloudy.) Add the liqueur, vanilla
extract, and salt to the berry sauce.

4 In a deep, 4-quart saucepan, combine 1¼ cups of the berry sauce (reserve any extra to spoon over ice cream) and the remaining 2 cups of granulated sugar. Bring to a boil over medium-high heat, stirring to dissolve the sugar. Boil for 6 minutes, stirring occasionally, as the mixture will foam up. To keep the mixture from boiling over, decrease the heat while still maintaining a steady boil.

5 While the mixture is boiling, use scissors to cut the tops from the pouches of pectin. Stand the pouches in a glass measure to keep them from tipping over.

6 Remove the pan from the heat and immediately stir in the pouches of pectin until completely combined.

7 Quickly pour the mixture into the prepared pan, covering the bottom of the pan completely and evenly. Do not stir, touch, or wiggle the pan, as the sauce jells very quickly and you want the surface to be completely smooth. Set the pan aside in a cool, dry spot to set, about 3 hours or up to 12 hours.

8 Place about 1 cup of the superfine sugar on a plate. Set aside. Place a sheet of parchment paper on a large cutting board.

9 Run a knife along the edges of the pan to loosen the sides of the jelly. Invert the jelly onto the parchment paper. Carefully remove the sheet of parchment from the topside of the jelly. Use a ruler and long, thin-bladed sharp knife to measure and cut the jellies into 1-inch squares. Rinse and dry the knife as needed to keep it clean. Gently lift the squares from the parchment and toss them in the sugar to coat all sides, gently dabbing any bare spots on the jellies with sugar. Transfer them to a clean, parchment-lined baking sheet. Repeat until all the jellies are coated.

STORING: *Store the jellies on a baking sheet covered with aluminum foil until ready to package. The jellies will keep at room temperature for 2 months.*

GIFT CARD: These handcrafted Blackberry-Merlot Jellies were made on [give date] and can be enjoyed for up to 2 months, but they won't last that long!

GIFT-GIVING TIPS: Wrap the jellies in small attractive tins or laminated gift boxes lined with parchment paper. Attach a gift card. To turn this into a gift basket, consider including petite cookies and chocolates to create a petit four sampler. An eau-de-vie or grappa would be a fun and generous addition.

TOASTED COCONUT MARSHMALLOWS

INGREDIENTS

2½ cups sweetened shredded
   coconut

¾ cup cold water

1¼ cups granulated sugar

2 tablespoons light corn syrup

2 (¼-ounce) packets unflavored
   gelatin

3 large egg whites, at room
   temperature

1 tablespoon pure vanilla extract

IMPLEMENTS

Measuring Cups and Spoons, Large
Rimmed Baking Sheet, Silicone
Spatula, Parchment Paper, 12 by
8 by 1-Inch Jellyroll Pan, Medium
Saucepan, Wooden Spoon, Candy
Thermometer, Small Microwave-
Safe Bowl, Stand Mixer with Whip
Attachment or Hand Mixer, Rubber
Spatula, Ruler, Long Thin-Bladed
Sharp Knife, Medium Bowl

In Dorie Greenspan's luscious recipe for marshmallows in her cookbook *Baking: From My Home to Yours*, she suggests "playing around" with the marshmallow recipe and offers several variations. Inspired by her, we took the liberty to play around and came up with our own—a lofty and light marshmallow completely coated with toasted shredded coconut. It is a childhood love for coconut, especially toasted coconut, that led us to adapt her recipe. It's playtime in the kitchen, and sweet treats to give are the result.

Prep Time: 20 minutes | Cook Time: 25 minutes total | Set Time: 3 hours |
Makes forty (1¼-inch-square) marshmallows

1 Position a rack in the center of the oven. Preheat the oven to 300°F.

2 Spread the coconut in an even layer on a large rimmed baking sheet. Toast the coconut, stirring every 3 minutes, until it is rich golden brown, about 12 minutes. (Stirring frequently will ensure even browning and also prevent the coconut from burning at the edges of the pan.) Remove from the oven and set aside.

3 Meanwhile, cut a rectangle of parchment paper to fit the bottom of a 12 by 8 by 1-inch jellyroll pan. Spread ¾ cup of the toasted coconut in an even layer on the parchment. Set the pan aside and reserve the rest of the coconut.

4 Combine ⅓ cup of the water, the sugar, and corn syrup in a medium saucepan. Bring to a boil over medium heat, stirring to dissolve the sugar. Once the sugar has dissolved, cook the syrup without stirring until the mixture reaches 265°F on a candy thermometer, 8 to 10 minutes.

5   While the syrup is cooking, prepare the gelatin. In a small, microwave-safe bowl, sprinkle the gelatin over the remaining water, tilting the bowl a bit to wet all of the gelatin granules. Let it sit until spongy, about 5 minutes. Warm the gelatin in a microwave to liquefy it, about 20 seconds. Set aside.

6   Put the egg whites in the bowl of a stand mixer fitted with the whisk attachment or in a large bowl with a hand mixer. When the sugar syrup is just below 265°F, begin beating the egg whites on medium-high speed until glossy with soft peaks. Turn the mixer off momentarily.

7   Once the sugar syrup reaches 265°F, remove the pan from the heat, turn the mixer to medium speed, and pour the sugar syrup in a slow, steady stream down along the sides of the bowl. Beat until all the syrup is incorporated, and then slowly pour the gelatin mixture into the egg whites. Beat for 3 minutes. Add the vanilla and beat, scraping down the sides of the bowl once with a rubber spatula, until incorporated, 30 seconds longer.

8   Using a rubber spatula, lift globs of the marshmallow mixture and gently plop them on the coconut, without disturbing the coconut. Cover the coconut with these mounds, and then use a rubber spatula to gently spread them into an even layer. The marshmallow mixture should be even with the top of the jellyroll pan. Evenly and generously sprinkle ¾ cup of the reserved coconut over the top of the marshmallows. Set the pan aside in a cool, dry spot to set, about 3 hours or up to 12 hours.

9   Use a ruler and long, thin-bladed sharp knife to measure and cut the marshmallows into 1¼-inch squares. Rinse and dry the knife as needed to keep it clean. Put the remaining toasted coconut in a medium bowl. Gently lift the marshmallow squares from the parchment and toss them in the coconut to coat all sides, gently pressing coconut onto any bare spots. Transfer them to a clean baking sheet. Repeat until all the marshmallows are coated.

STORING: *Store the marshmallows on a baking sheet covered with aluminum foil until ready to package. The marshmallows will keep at room temperature for 1 week.*

GIFT CARD: These Toasted Coconut Marshmallows are, of course, fabulous to eat out of hand, and the box may be gone before you know it, but these are also downright decadent when made into s'mores or added to hot chocolate!

GIFT-GIVING TIPS: Wrap the marshmallows in small attractive tins or laminated gift boxes lined with decorative waxed paper, or stack them in cellophane bags and tie them with a ribbon. Attach a gift card. To turn this into a gift basket, consider including the Cinnamon-Coated Graham Crackers on page 113 or store-bought graham crackers, 2 bars of semisweet or dark chocolate, a jar of rich-tasting chocolate sauce, and the recipe for S'Mores without a Campfire on page 114.

CHIPOTLE CHILE CANDIED PECANS

INGREDIENTS

½ cup (1 stick) unsalted butter

1 teaspoon ground chipotle chile powder

1 cup packed light brown sugar

1 teaspoon pure vanilla extract

2 large egg whites, at room temperature

¾ teaspoon kosher or sea salt

1 pound large or jumbo pecan halves

IMPLEMENTS

Large Rimmed Nonstick Baking Sheet, Measuring Cups and Spoons, Small Bowl, Stand Mixer with Whip Attachment or Hand Mixer, Rubber Spatula

These candied pecans are flat-out decadent and irresistible. Sweet, spicy, with a hint of salt, these meringue-sugar-crusted pecans are divine eaten out of hand with a tumbler of bourbon or Scotch. However, a handful of these nuts tossed into a mesclun salad along with sweetened dried cranberries and crumbled blue cheese is the perfect starter to a holiday meal. This recipe can easily be doubled; use two baking sheets with a stick of butter melted on each, and whip the double batch of meringue in a stand mixer or large mixing bowl.

Prep Time: 20 minutes | Active Bake Time: about 1¼ hours, stirring every 15 minutes | Makes 1 pound nuts, portioned into four (¼-pound) packages

1 Position a rack in the center of the oven. Preheat the oven to 300°F. Have ready a large rimmed baking sheet, preferably nonstick for easier cleanup.

2 Melt the butter on the baking sheet in the oven. Be careful not to let the butter brown. Set aside.

3 Combine the chile powder and brown sugar in a small bowl. Pour the vanilla over the brown sugar. Set aside.

4 In the bowl of a stand mixer fitted with the whisk attachment, beat the egg whites on medium speed until foamy. Add ¼ teaspoon of salt and beat on medium-high speed until soft peaks form. Add the sugar mixture 2 tablespoons at a time, beating on high speed to form a strong, shiny meringue. Remove the bowl from the mixer and use a rubber spatula to gently fold in the nuts until they are well coated.

5 Gently tip the rimmed baking sheet so the butter coats the bottom of the pan. Using a rubber spatula, spread the nuts over the butter, without stirring, to form an even layer without deflating the meringue.

6 Bake the nuts for 20 minutes. Remove them from the oven and stir the nuts with a spatula, moving the nuts at the center of the pan to the edges and the nuts at the edges closer to the center. Return the pan to the oven, bake the nuts for 15 minutes longer, and stir them again. Sprinkle the nuts with the remaining ½ teaspoon of salt.

7 Continue baking, stirring every 15 minutes, until the nuts are separated, have absorbed the butter and glisten, and are beautifully browned, 45 minutes to 1 hour longer.

8 Immediately turn the nuts out onto a counter lined with a long sheet of aluminum foil, spread them out, and let cool completely.

RECIPE CARD: CREATE A CARD TO PACKAGE WITH GIFT

CHIPOTLE CHILE CANDIED PECAN, DRIED CRANBERRY, AND CRUMBLED BLUE CHEESE SALAD

Combine a handful of these candied pecans, along with ¼ cup of sweetened dried cranberries and ½ cup of crumbled blue cheese, with 8 cups of loosely packed mesclun greens. Toss with your favorite vinaigrette and serve. Add thin slices of crisp apples or ripe pears, if desired.

STORING: *Store in a tightly covered tin or covered glass container. The nuts will keep for up to 3 weeks.*

GIFT-GIVING TIPS: Wrap the nuts in small attractive tins or laminated gift boxes lined with decorative waxed paper. To turn this into a gift basket, consider including a bottle of bourbon or Scotch—a perfect accompaniment! Alternatively, pack a gift basket or lovely salad bowl with the nuts, sweetened dried cranberries, crumbled blue cheese, and a recipe card for the salad below.

ROASTED WHITE CHOCOLATE–DIPPED APPLES

INGREDIENTS

1 (8.82-ounce) bar Valrhona white
chocolate (Blanc 35 percent)

½ teaspoon fine sea salt

6 large or 8 medium firm, very crisp
apples, such as Braeburn, Gala,
or Golden Delicious, at room
temperature

IMPLEMENTS

Shallow 2-Quart Baking Dish,
Kitchen Timer, Silicone Spatula,
Measuring Spoons, Sturdy Rimmed
Baking Sheet, Six to Eight (4½ by
⅜-inch) Wooden Popsicle Sticks,
Parchment Paper

After a lengthy conversation about making truffles with Portland-based chocolatier David Briggs of Xocolatl de Davíd, he mentioned roasting white chocolate until it turned a luscious caramel color and using it as the center for truffles. We were intrigued; more precisely, we became obsessed. We're not sure we have ever tested and re-tested a technique and recipe as much as this one, but the results are spectacular. Once we mastered the roasting technique, we played in the kitchen, thinking up all sorts of ways to use the chocolate—and dipping apples came to mind. Step aside, caramel-coated apples—there is a new decadent treat in town. Use high-quality white chocolate; in our experience, this recipe works best with Valrhona Blanc 35 percent. As the chocolate roasts, it will look grainy and even clump, but with frequent stirring it smoothes out until it is silky and creamy—the texture is simply incomparable. Once the apples are coated and placed in the refrigerator to allow the chocolate to set, the coating will turn whitish, and then after about 24 hours it turns back to the original rich caramel color.

Prep Time: 5 minutes | Roasting Time: about 1¾ hours | Set Time: 24 hours |
Makes six large or eight medium chocolate-covered apples

1 Position a rack in the center of the oven. Preheat the oven to 250°F. (Use an oven thermometer, if necessary, to make sure your oven is calibrated accurately.) Break the chocolate into small pieces and place in an even layer in a glass or ceramic baking dish.

2 Bake the chocolate for 1½ to 1¾ hours, stirring thoroughly every 10 minutes, until the chocolate is the color of peanut butter and has a nutty flavor. (Be sure to set a timer; it is critical to stir the chocolate every 10 minutes, as the bottom is what begins to brown first. We like to set a second timer for 90 minutes to help us keep track of the overall baking time.)

3 Set the baking pan on a hot pad or cotton towel. Add the salt to the chocolate and stir until it loosens up and becomes a silky consistency, about 5 minutes.

4 Twist to remove the stems from the apples and insert an ice-pop stick into the top of each apple. Have ready a rimmed baking sheet lined with parchment paper.

5 Working with one apple at a time, set the apple in the baking dish and, with the aid of a soup spoon, pour the melted chocolate over the apple, coating it completely. Lift the apple up and let the excess chocolate drip back into the dish. Transfer the coated apple to the prepared baking sheet. Repeat to coat all the apples.

6 Refrigerate the apples until the chocolate is set and completely hardened, 24 hours.

STORING: *Refrigerate for up to 10 days.*

GIFT CARD: This handcrafted Roasted White Chocolate–Dipped Apple was made on [give date] and can be enjoyed for up to 1 week, stored in the refrigerator.

GIFT-GIVING TIPS: Cut clear cellophane wrap into 13-inch squares. Set the apple in the center of the cellophane square, gather up the sides, and secure at the top with raffia or ribbon. Attach a gift card.

SMOKED SALT, DRIED APRICOT, AND ALMOND CHOCOLATE BARK

INGREDIENTS

½ cup dry roasted unsalted almonds, coarsely chopped

⅔ cup chopped dried apricots

1 pound bittersweet chocolate (at least 64 percent cacao), finely chopped

1½ to 2 teaspoons coarse-ground smoked salt

IMPLEMENTS

17 by 11-Inch Baking Sheet, Parchment Paper, Measuring Cups, Chef's Knife, Cutting Board, Medium Bowl, Large Microwave-Safe Bowl or Double Boiler, Rubber Spatula, Instant-Read Thermometer, Offset Spatula

While chocolate truffles are fun to make for holiday gift giving, they do require several steps, including a chill time in order for the ganache to set. Chocolate bark, on the other hand, can be a quick spur-of-the-moment project, and only a few tools are needed. In particular, you'll need an instant-read thermometer in order to properly temper the chocolate; a narrow, long-bladed offset spatula that allows you to smoothly and evenly spread the chocolate; and some parchment paper to line a baking sheet.

This recipe is divine with the crunch of nuts, the orange pop of color from the fruit, and the tantalizing hint of salt. However, it is also fun to experiment with different flavor combinations while following the same method and keeping the same proportions. Consider using pistachios, roasted hazelnuts, macadamia nuts, pumpkin seeds, dried cherries or cranberries, finely chopped crystallized ginger, or even crushed peppermint patties. Giving food gifts is all about having fun in the kitchen, and this chocolate bark is certainly a delight to make.

Prep Time: 15 minutes | Cook Time: 4 minutes | Set Time: 1 hour | Makes 1 pound of chocolate bark, portioned into four (¼-pound) packages

1 Line a 17 by 11-inch baking sheet with parchment paper. Combine the almonds and dried apricots in a medium bowl.

2 The chocolate can be tempered either using a microwave oven (the easiest way) or on the stovetop in a double boiler. To temper the chocolate using a microwave, place three-quarters of the chopped chocolate in a microwave-safe glass or ceramic bowl. Set aside the remaining chocolate. Set the microwave at 50 percent power. With the bowl uncovered, heat the chocolate for 1 minute, and then stir using a rubber spatula. Repeat,

heating for 30 seconds and then stirring, until almost all of the chocolate in the bowl is melted, about 4 minutes total. To temper chocolate on the stovetop in a double boiler, place three-quarters of the chocolate in the top of a double boiler over barely simmering water. (Check to make sure the water doesn't touch the top section of the double boiler, and be careful that no water drips into the bowl of chocolate.)

3 Using an instant-read thermometer, check the temperature of the chocolate. It should be about 115°F. Heat briefly if it hasn't reached the desired temperature. Then add the remaining chocolate and stir constantly until it is completely melted and smooth and the chocolate drops to just below 84°F. At this point, very slowly and carefully heat the chocolate, bringing the temperature of the chocolate back up to 88° to 90°F. The chocolate is now tempered and ready to spread.

4 Working quickly and using an offset spatula, spread the chocolate in an even layer about ¼ inch thick on the parchment. Evenly and artfully scatter the apricots and almonds over the chocolate. With a delicate touch, use your fingertips to gently press the nuts and apricots into the chocolate so they set into and adhere to the chocolate.

5 Immediately sprinkle the salt over the top. Set the bark aside in a cool, dry spot to set and harden, about 1 hour. Break into irregular pieces.

STORING: *Store in a tightly covered tin lined with parchment paper. The chocolate bark will last for up to 3 weeks.*

GIFT CARD: This handcrafted Smoked Salt, Dried Apricot, and Almond Chocolate Bark was made on [give date] and can be enjoyed for up to 1 month when stored in a cool, dry place.

GIFT-GIVING TIPS: Wrap the chocolate bark in gift boxes or airtight tins lined with decorative waxed paper or parchment paper. Alternatively, arrange the bark in cellophane bags and tie with a ribbon. Attach a gift card. To turn this into a gift basket, consider including a bottle of port or brandy.

CHAPTER 10

DRINK *gifts*

Skoal! Be the toast of the town when you give these ambrosia-like drink gifts. We predict you'll feel like a sorcerer concocting these potions, and your wizardry will be greeted with audible gasps of awe and wonder. So put on that apron emblazoned with stars and moons, and make some summertime berry-basil margarita purée, Italian liqueurs, or drinking chocolate magic.

LIMONCELLO

INGREDIENTS

15 organic lemons

2 (750-milliliter) bottles 151- or 190-proof grain alcohol, such as Everclear (see page 11)

4 cups granulated sugar

9½ cups water

IMPLEMENTS

1-Gallon Glass Jar, Vegetable Peeler, Long Wooden Spoon, Measuring Cups, Large Saucepan, Four (1-Liter) Glass Bottles, Fine-Mesh Strainer or Coffee Filter, Large Bowl, Narrow-Neck Funnel, Ladle

The saying goes, "When life hands you lemons, make lemonade." We say, "When you are handed lemons, make limoncello and lemonade." It takes 15 lemons to make limoncello, and since only the peel is used, that leaves all the fruit to juice for a refreshingly large pitcher of homemade lemonade—that's the beauty of making limoncello in the summer! In addition, since it takes 40 to 80 days for the mixture to infuse, if you make it over the summer you'll have bottles of limoncello ready for holiday gift giving. Use the freshest, most blemish-free, most fully ripe lemons you can find. In addition, buy organic ones if possible. Since the limoncello is made from the lemon peel, you want to make sure they haven't been coated or sprayed with pesticides.

Prep Time: 15 minutes | Infusing Time: 40 to 80 days | Makes four (1-liter) bottles of limoncello

1 Wash a 1-gallon glass jar and lid in hot, soapy water and dry thoroughly. Alternatively, run the jar and lid through the regular cycle of your dishwasher.

2 Scrub the lemons in warm water and pat dry. Using a vegetable peeler, remove the peel from each lemon in wide strips. Be careful not to remove the white pith, which will impart a bitter flavor to the limoncello.

3 Place the lemon peels in the prepared jar. Pour in 1 bottle of the alcohol, and push down the lemon peels with a wooden spoon to completely submerge them in the liquid. Tightly secure the lid, and set the jar in a cool, dark place to steep. Stirring is not necessary.

4 After 20 or 40 days, add the second bottle of alcohol to the mixture. Place the sugar and 7½ cups of the water in a large saucepan and bring to a boil over high heat, stirring to dissolve the sugar. Decrease to a simmer and cook for 10 minutes to ensure that all the sugar is completely dissolved. Remove from the heat and cool.

5 When the sugar syrup is completely cool, add it to the lemon and alcohol mixture in the jar. Tightly secure the lid, and return the jar to a cool, dark place to steep for an additional 20 to 40 days. Over time, the liquid will absorb the flavor from the lemon peels and turn bright yellow in color.

6 To bottle, first wash the bottles in hot, soapy water and dry thoroughly. Alternatively, run the bottles through the regular cycle of your dishwasher.

7 Strain the liquid through a fine-mesh strainer, or coffee filter set in a strainer, into a large bowl. Add 1⅔ cups of water to the limencello if you used 151-proof grain alcohol; add 2 cups of water if you used 190-proof. (Note: The addition of the water will turn the liquid cloudy and pale yellow in color. This is the desired outcome.) Let it rest for a moment so that any remaining sediment will fall to the bottom of the bowl.

8 Using a narrow-neck funnel, ladle the limoncello into the prepared bottles, leaving 1 inch headspace. Wipe the rims clean, secure the lids, and label.

STORING: *Store the bottles in a cool, dark place, or keep in the freezer until ready to serve. Limoncello will keep for several years.*

GIFT CARD: This homemade Limoncello was bottled on [give date] and can be enjoyed for several years to come. Store it in the freezer, and enjoy it as a refreshing liqueur to sip after dinner.

GIFT-GIVING TIPS: Tie each bottle with raffia or ribbon and attach a gift card. To turn this into a gift basket, add a set of cordial glasses.

MEXICAN DRINKING CHOCOLATE

INGREDIENTS

1¼ pounds (20 ounces) bittersweet chocolate (61 to 66 percent cacao), finely chopped

2¼ cups heavy (whipping) cream

2 soft, plump whole vanilla beans, split and scraped

2 teaspoons ground cinnamon

½ teaspoon ground chipotle chile powder

¼ cup light corn syrup

½ teaspoon almond extract

IMPLEMENTS

Four (½-Pint) Decorative Glass Jars with Tight-Fitting Lids, Kitchen Scale, Cutting Board, Chef's Knife, Large Heatproof Glass or Stainless-Steel Bowl, Measuring Cups and Spoons, Paring Knife, Medium Saucepan, Silicone Spatula

Irresistible, especially on a cold winter's day, this hot chocolate drink is deeply rich, vanilla-perfumed, and chile-charged—an ideal gift for friends who ski, snowboard, or ice skate. You make the decadent base, pour it into jars, and refrigerate until it sets like a firm ganache. Tie the decorative jars with ribbon and attach a recipe card. Spooned from the jar into a warm mug, the chocolate is stirred with hot or steamed milk for an indulgent, après-ski treat by the fire—a cozy, delicious gift.

Prep Time: 20 minutes | Cook Time: 5 minutes | Makes four (½-pint) jars of drinking chocolate

1 Wash the jars, including the lids, in hot, soapy water and dry thoroughly. Alternatively, run the jars through the regular cycle of your dishwasher; wash the lids by hand.

2 Place the chocolate in a large heatproof bowl. Set aside.

3 In a medium saucepan over low heat, bring the cream, vanilla beans (seeds and pods), cinnamon, and chipotle chile to a boil, stirring frequently. Remove from the heat. Using a silicone spatula, press the vanilla pods against the side of the pan to remove any remaining seeds and cream. Discard the pods.

4 Immediately pour the cream mixture over the chocolate, stirring constantly until the chocolate is completely melted and smooth. Add the corn syrup and almond extract, stirring until incorporated.

5 Pour the chocolate ganache into the prepared jars, dividing it evenly and leaving ½ inch headspace. Wipe the rims clean and secure the lids. Label and refrigerate.

RECIPE CARD: CREATE A CARD TO PACKAGE WITH GIFT

MEXICAN HOT CHOCOLATE

This homemade Mexican Drinking Chocolate was made on [give date] and can be enjoyed for up to 2 weeks. To make a cup of drinking chocolate, use a spoon that has been warmed under hot water to scoop and measure ¼ cup of the chocolate into a preheated mug. Add ½ cup of hot or steamed milk and stir until the chocolate is completely melted and smooth. Top with a dollop of whipped cream and sprinkle a little cocoa powder over the top. Serve immediately.

STORING: *Refrigerate for up to 2 weeks.*

GIFT-GIVING TIPS: Tie each jar with raffia or ribbon and attach a recipe card. To turn this into a gift basket, consider including small mugs or even cappuccino cups and saucers, along with a fine-mesh shaker filled with a specialty cocoa powder for dusting the top of the drinks.

BLUEBERRY-BLACKBERRY-BASIL MARGARITA PURÉE

INGREDIENTS

½ cup granulated sugar

¼ cup water

½ cup lightly packed fresh basil
leaves

3 cups fresh blueberries

3 cups fresh blackberries

¼ cup freshly squeezed lime juice

2 tablespoons freshly squeezed
lemon juice

IMPLEMENTS

Two (¾-Liter) Glass Canning Jars
with Airtight Clamp Lids, Measuring
Cup and Spoons, Small Saucepan,
Wooden Spoon, Fine-Mesh Strainer,
Blender, Juicer, Medium Bowl,
Rubber Spatula, Wide-Mouth
Funnel, Ladle

It's gift-giving time and party time all in one. Consider this gift as "summer in a glass"—an easy-to-make combo of blended, strained blueberries and blackberries, given an herbal twist with basil-infused simple syrup. To add a cool touch, as well as whimsy and fun, to a backyard party, blend this margarita base together with premium silver tequila and a touch of Cointreau in an ice-cream maker. The results are berrylicious—an adult slushie—ready for a chilled margarita glass rimmed with sugar and garnished with a wheel of lime.

Prep Time: 30 minutes | Makes two (¾-liter) jars of margarita purée; each jar is enough for four margaritas

1   Wash the jars in hot, soapy water and dry thoroughly. Alternatively, run the jars through the regular cycle of your dishwasher; wash the rubber gaskets by hand.

2   Combine the sugar and water in a small saucepan and bring to a boil over medium-high heat, stirring to dissolve the sugar. Add the basil, decrease the heat, and simmer for 2 minutes. Remove the pan from the heat and set aside to cool. Using a fine-mesh strainer, strain the simple syrup into a blender. Discard the basil.

3   Add the blueberries, blackberries, and lime and lemon juices to the blender. Holding the blender lid securely in place, blend the mixture on high speed until puréed. Using a fine-mesh strainer set over a medium bowl, strain the berry purée to remove all the seeds. Using a rubber spatula, press down to extract all the purée. Discard the seeds.

4 Using a wide-mouth funnel and filling one jar at a time, ladle the berry purée into the prepared jars, leaving 1 inch headspace. Wipe the rims clean and secure the lids. Label and refrigerate.

RECIPE CARD: CREATE A CARD TO PACKAGE WITH GIFT

BLUEBERRY-BLACKBERRY-BASIL MARGARITAS

This Blueberry-Blackberry-Basil Purée was made on [give date] and can be enjoyed for up to 10 days, kept in the refrigerator, or 3 months if frozen. To make the margaritas, combine the berry purée with ½ cup water, 2 ounces premium silver tequila, and 2 ounces Cointreau in the freezer bowl of an ice-cream maker. Churn the mixture until it reaches a slushy consistency, about 10 minutes. Pour into sugar-rimmed margarita glasses and garnish with a wheel of lime. Serves 4.

STORING: *Refrigerate for up to 10 days, or freeze for up to 3 months.*

GIFT-GIVING TIPS: Tie each jar with raffia or ribbon and attach a recipe card. To turn this into a gift basket, include a bottle of premium silver tequila, such as Don Julio, and a bottle of Cointreau. To make the gift a bit more elaborate, add a set of margarita glasses.

ITALIAN NOCINO LIQUEUR

INGREDIENTS

30 fresh green walnuts with soft shells (picked in late spring/early summer; see page 13)

1 (750-milliliter) bottle 151- or 190-proof grain alcohol, such as Everclear (see page 11)

1 (750-milliliter) bottle inexpensive white wine, such as pinot grigio

4 cups granulated sugar

Peel from 1 lemon (yellow part without the white pith)

40 whole cloves

3 (3-inch-long) cinnamon sticks

IMPLEMENTS

1-Gallon Glass Jar, Cutting Board, Chef's Knife, Measuring Cup, Vegetable Peeler, Long Wooden Spoon, Nine (7- to 8-Ounce) Glass Bottles, Colander, Large Bowl, Large Pitcher, Fine-Mesh Strainer, Coffee Filters, Narrow-Neck Funnel

You don't need a walnut tree in your backyard or your neighbor's to make nocino. Who knew, but you can even order green walnuts online, in season (www.localharvest.org). This Italian liqueur, made from unripe walnuts, is traditionally started in late June, when the walnut shells are still green and soft, like little limes. For 5 months the green walnuts, along with whole spices, lemon peel, and sugar, soak in a bath of grain alcohol and white wine. By the holiday season, the liquid has turned a deep, rich brown and is ready for bottling—just in time for gift giving.

Prep Time: 15 minutes | Infusing Time: 5 months | Bottling Time: 30 minutes | Makes nine (7- to 8-ounce) bottles of nocino

1 Wash a 1-gallon glass jar and lid in hot, soapy water and dry thoroughly. Alternatively, run the jar and lid through the regular cycle of your dishwasher.

2 Scrub the walnuts in warm water and pat dry. Quarter the walnuts and place them in the prepared jar. Add the alcohol, wine, sugar, lemon peel, cloves, and cinnamon sticks. Cover the jar and tightly secure the lid. Set the jar in front of a window to steep in sunlight for about 5 months. Shake the jar once a week. Over time, the liquid will turn deep, dark brown in color.

3 To bottle, first wash the bottles in hot, soapy water and dry thoroughly. Alternatively, run the bottles through the regular cycle of your dishwasher.

4 Set a colander over a large bowl and strain the liquid to remove the walnuts, peels, and whole spices. Discard the solids. Set a fine-mesh strainer over a large pitcher and strain the liquid to remove the large bits of sediment. Rinse and dry the strainer and the bowl.

5 Line the strainer with a coffee filter and set it over the bowl. Strain the liquid through the filter, removing yet more sediment. Pour the nocino from the bowl back into the large pitcher.

6 Using a funnel lined with a clean coffee filter, pour the nocino into the prepared bottles, leaving ½ inch headspace. Wipe the rims clean, secure the lids, and label.

STORING: *Store the bottles in a cool, dark place. Nocino will keep for several years.*

GIFT CARD: This homemade Italian Nocino Liqueur was bottled on [give date] and can be enjoyed for several years to come. Enjoy it as a sipping liqueur, drizzled over vanilla bean ice cream, or for dipping biscotti.

GIFT-GIVING TIPS: Tie each bottle with raffia or ribbon and attach a gift card. To turn this into a gift basket, add a set of cordial glasses.

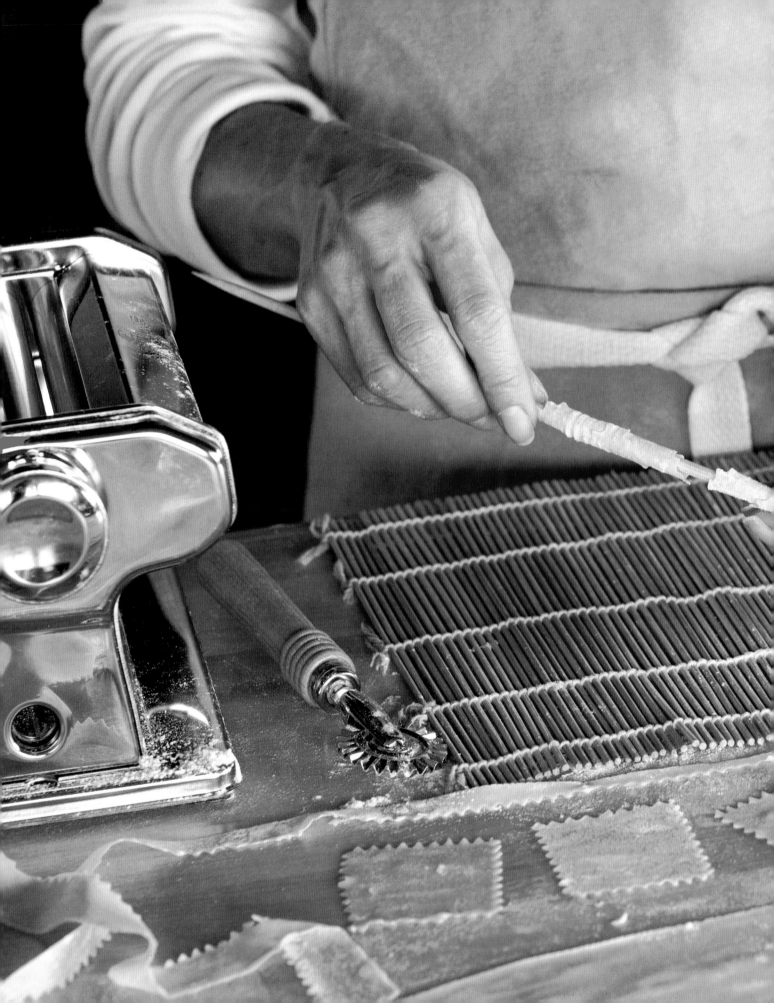

CHAPTER 11

NO-COOK *gifts*

No need to light a burner or heat the oven to make an amazing culinary treat. The most discerning foodies on your list will warmly receive these outstanding no-cook gifts. Homemade butter? Talk about the "Wow!" factor. And the best part is that you don't have to use any magic to make it. Other sure-to-please, no-cook goodies come loaded with rich, captivating aromas, including homemade vanilla extract, a Moroccan spice blend, and sweet and savory popcorn seasoning.

HOME-CHURNED LEMON-HERB BUTTER

INGREDIENTS

1 pint heavy (whipping) cream, preferably not ultrapasteurized

1 tablespoon finely chopped fresh tarragon

1 tablespoon finely chopped fresh dill

1 tablespoon finely chopped fresh chives

1 tablespoon finely chopped fresh flat-leaf parsley

1 teaspoon minced lemon zest (about 1 lemon)

½ teaspoon kosher or sea salt

IMPLEMENTS

Measuring Cups and Spoons, Stand Mixer with Paddle Attachment, Rubber Spatula, Strainer, Medium Bowl, Cheesecloth or Lint-Free Kitchen Towel, Plate, Table Knife, Cutting Board, Chef's Knife, Zester, Two (½-Cup) Butter Bells (Optional)

How is this for gift-giving fun—churning your own butter from cream and turning it into herb butter? That's homemade! And it is spectacularly easy. Start with high-quality cream, preferably not ultra-pasteurized. The liquid (whey) that separates from the butter solids during churning is not sour like buttermilk because acid is not added in this process, the way commercial creameries do. It can't be used in recipes that call for buttermilk; however, the whey can be used as you would reduced-fat milk—it's delicious with cereal or homemade granola! (See page 100.) The lemon-herb butter is terrific simply spread on bread, melted and tossed with popcorn, softened and rubbed on a chicken before roasting, melted to fry an egg or make an omelet, or spooned into a baked potato.

Churn Time: 15 minutes | Chill Time: 1 hour | Prep Time: 20 minutes | Makes 1 cup of butter, enough to fill two (½-cup) butter bells

1 In the bowl of a stand mixer fitted with the paddle attachment, churn the cream on medium speed until the butter solids separate from the liquid, about 15 minutes. Occasionally stop the mixer to scrape down the sides of the bowl with a rubber spatula. (As it churns, the cream will go through stages—from whipped cream to pea-size clumps to large hunks of golden yellow butter with liquid whey pooled in the bottom of the mixer.)

2 To separate the butter and whey, transfer the mixture to a mesh strainer set over a medium bowl. Pour the whey into a covered container and refrigerate, reserving it for another use (see headnote).

3 Place the butter in the bowl and fill the bowl with cold water. Gently massage the butter in the water to remove the excess whey from the surface of the butter. Pour out the water and refill the bowl with fresh cold water. Repeat this process until the water runs clear.

4 Wrap the butter in a triple layer of cheesecloth or a clean kitchen towel and form it into a flattened disk. Put the butter on a plate and place it in the refrigerator for at least 1 hour to chill and allow excess moisture to seep out and absorb into the cheesecloth.

5 Remove the chilled butter from the cheesecloth and gently scrape the surface with the back of a table knife to remove any residue from the cloth. Cut the butter into large cubes and place them in the bowl of a stand mixer fitted with the paddle attachment. Add the tarragon, dill, chives, parsley, lemon zest, and salt. Cream the mixture together on low speed for 1 to 2 minutes. Divide the lemon-herb butter between 2 butter bells, packing the butter into the containers and smoothing the tops. Cover and refrigerate. Alternatively, separate the butter into 2 equal hunks, wrap them in plastic wrap. and form them into 1½-inch-diameter rolls. Wrap each roll in parchment paper, twist and tie the ends to seal, and refrigerate.

Note: If you'd rather not make butter from scratch, combine 1 cup (2 sticks) of softened unsalted butter with the herbs and lemon zest in a mixer fitted with the paddle attachment. Mix until thoroughly combined. (Whether you start with cream and churn your own butter, or begin with butter, this recipe can easily be doubled to make four gifts.)

STORING: *Refrigerate for up to 2 weeks or freeze for up to 3 months.*

GIFT CARD: This Home-Churned Lemon-Herb Butter was made on [give date] and can be enjoyed for up to 2 weeks, kept in the refrigerator, or up to 3 months if frozen. It is delightful rubbed on chicken before roasting, melted over freshly popped popcorn, spooned over a baked potato, or simply spread on warm dinner rolls.

GIFT-GIVING TIPS: Tie each butter bell or parchment-wrapped butter roll with raffia or ribbon and attach a gift card. To turn this into a gift basket, see the Retro Popcorn Gift Kit on page 173.

BOLLYWOOD COCONUT CURRY POPCORN SEASONING

INGREDIENTS

1¾ cups sweetened shredded coconut

7 tablespoons Madras curry powder

3½ teaspoons granulated sugar

2 tablespoons kosher or sea salt

1¾ teaspoons ground ginger

1¾ teaspoons ground cinnamon

1 teaspoon cayenne pepper

1 teaspoon garlic powder

IMPLEMENTS

Food Processor, Measuring Cups and Spoons, Three Spice Jars or Tins

This is popcorn for grown-ups! And what a great gift to give to college-age friends or family, young couples, or those married with children who are staying in for a date night. (Suggest on their gift card to pop in a movie and pop up some fresh popcorn once the kids are off to bed.) This fiery curry seasoning adds zest, spice, and sweetness to either freshly popped kernels or the microwave variety. It is essential to first drizzle melted butter over the popcorn and then toss it with some of the sweet and savory blend of curry powder, coconut, and other aromatic spices. This way, the seasoning sticks to each hot kernel. With a kick of heat, this is definitely an adult treat.

Prep Time: 20 minutes | Makes about 2 cups popcorn seasoning, enough to fill three (5- to 6-ounce) spice jars

1   In a food processor fitted with the metal blade, pulverize the coconut into tiny bits, 1 to 2 minutes. Add the curry powder, sugar, salt, ginger, cinnamon, cayenne, and garlic powder. Pulse to combine.

2   Divide into ¾-cup portions and transfer to jars or tins with tight-fitting lids.

STORING: *Store the popcorn seasoning away from heat and light for up to 4 months.*

GIFT CARD: This Bollywood Coconut Curry Popcorn Seasoning was blended on [give date] and can be enjoyed for up to 4 months. Generously sprinkle it over freshly popped popcorn coated with melted butter. It can also be tossed with microwave popcorn; just be sure to drizzle it with melted butter so the seasoning clings to each kernel!

GIFT-GIVING TIPS: Tie each jar or tin with raffia or ribbon and attach a gift card. To turn this into a gift basket, consider including popcorn kernels. To make the gift more elaborate, see page 173 for a Retro Popcorn Gift Kit idea.

MOROCCAN SPICE BLEND

INGREDIENTS

½ cup ground ginger

½ cup ground cumin

¼ cup *Pimentón de la Vera Dulce* (sweet smoked paprika)

¼ cup cayenne pepper

¼ cup ground cinnamon

¼ cup turmeric

¼ cup freshly ground black pepper

3 grams saffron threads, finely crushed

IMPLEMENTS

Medium Bowl, Measuring Cups, Whisk, Three Spice Jars or Tins

With nothing more than a bowl, whisk, and set of measuring cups, you can stir together a deliriously exotic spice blend, pack it into spice jars, and like magic have a unique gift for the cooks in your life. This aromatic mix of nine essential spices used in Moroccan cuisine can be the basis for a chicken or lamb tagine. Used as a rub, grilled pork tenderloin or chops get a power surge of flavor and ho-hum potatoes are deliciously vibrant when seasoned and roasted.

Prep Time: 20 minutes | Makes 2¼ cups of spice blend, enough to fill three (5- to 6-ounce) spice jars

1 In a medium bowl, whisk together the ginger, cumin, paprika, cayenne, cinnamon, turmeric, pepper, and saffron.

2 Divide into ¾-cup portions and transfer to jars or tins with tight-fitting lids.

PICTURED, TOP TO BOTTOM: BACKYARD BBQ RUB, MOROCCAN SPICE BLEND, BOLLYWOOD COCONUT CURRY POPCORN SEASONING

RECIPE CARD: CREATE A CARD TO PACKAGE WITH GIFT

CHICKEN TAGINE WITH OLIVES AND PRESERVED LEMON

Buy a cut-up chicken or cut a whole chicken into eighths, and generously season with kosher or sea salt. Rub the pieces with some of the Moroccan Spice Blend. In the base of a tagine or heavy skillet set over medium-high heat, melt 2 T. each of unsalted butter and olive oil. Brown the chicken on both sides, remove from the pan, and set aside. Decrease the heat to medium. Add 1½ cups thinly sliced onions and ¼ t. salt to the pan. Sauté, uncovered, until soft but not brown, about 5 minutes. Add 5 thinly sliced cloves of garlic, and sauté until the onions are translucent, 3 to 5 minutes longer. Pour in 1½ cups chicken broth and ⅓ cup orange juice. Return the chicken to the pan, skin side up. Decrease the heat and simmer, covered, until the chicken is tender and easily shreds with a fork, about 45 minutes. Stir in 1 thinly sliced preserved lemon, ½ cup pitted Moroccan olives, and ¼ cup chopped fresh cilantro. Heat through. Serve the chicken over cooked couscous studded with golden raisins and ladle the sauce around. Sprinkle with additional chopped cilantro to garnish. Serves 4.

STORING: *Store the spice rub away from heat and light for up to 4 months.*

GIFT-GIVING TIPS: Tie each jar or tin with raffia or ribbon and attach a recipe card. To turn this into a gift basket, consider including a jar of Moroccan olives, couscous, and preserved lemons. To make the gift more elaborate, include a tagine, presenting these ingredients underneath the dome.

BACKYARD BBQ RUB

INGREDIENTS

½ cup kosher or sea salt

½ cup packed dark brown sugar

⅓ cup ground cumin

¼ cup coarsely ground black pepper

¼ cup sweet paprika

¼ cup dried thyme, crushed

¼ cup chili powder

2 tablespoons ground coriander

4 teaspoons ground cinnamon

IMPLEMENTS

Medium Bowl, Measuring Cups and Spoons, Wooden Spoon, Three Spice Jars or Tins

This big-flavored spice blend is guaranteed to ignite great taste when rubbed on shrimp, scallops, chicken, beef, lamb, buffalo, or pork. This recipe yields about 2½ cups of the spice rub, which is a great quantity to divide and package for gift giving.

Prep Time: 20 minutes | Makes about 2½ cups of rub, enough to fill three (5- to 6-ounce) spice jars

1 In a medium bowl, combine the salt, sugar, cumin, pepper, paprika, thyme, chili powder, coriander, and cinnamon. Stir well to blend.

2 Divide into ¾-cup portions and transfer to jars or tins with tight-fitting lids.

RECIPE CARD: CREATE A CARD TO PACKAGE WITH GIFT

GRILLED PORK TENDERLOIN WITH BACKYARD BBQ RUB

Prepare a medium-hot fire in a charcoal or gas grill. Remove 2 pork tenderloins from the refrigerator 30 minutes before grilling. Place on a rimmed baking sheet. Rub on all sides with olive oil and then rub each tenderloin with 2 T. of the rub. Grill, turning to sear all sides, until the pork is cooked through, slightly pink at the center, and registers 145°F on an instant-read thermometer, about 10 minutes. Let it rest for 5 minutes, slice, and serve.

STORING: *Store the spice rub away from heat and light for up to 4 months.*

GIFT-GIVING TIPS: Tie each jar or tin with raffia or ribbon and attach a recipe card. To turn this into a gift basket, consider including some smoking chips, alder planks, or decorative metal grilling skewers. To make the gift a bit more elaborate, include a set of grill tools, a grill basket, or even long grill mitts.

HOMEMADE GARGANELLI

INGREDIENTS

5¼ cups (23½ ounces) tipo "00"
   flour or all-purpose flour, plus
   more for dusting (see page 15)
7 large eggs

IMPLEMENTS

Measuring Cups, Stand Mixer
with Paddle and Dough Hook
Attachment, Electric or Hand-Crank
Pasta Machine, Bench Scraper,
Ruler, Fluted Pastry Cutter, Bamboo
Sushi Mat(s), ½-Inch-Thick Wooden
Dowel About 10 Inches Long, Two
Large Flour Sack Towels

Here's a treasured gift given with a big Italian hug—
whether you are Italian or not! Homemade pasta,
especially rustic-shaped garganelli, is as much fun to
make as it is to give. It's a perfect present to make any
time of year, and it gives you a lazy day to play in the
kitchen. Although this might raise the hairs on the back
of a nonna's neck, my secret to getting the fine ridges in
the pasta is to use a bamboo sushi mat! The traditional
wooden garganelli comb is hard to find outside of Italy, and
the sushi mat works brilliantly, with enough surface area
to roll two garganelli at once. You'll need to buy a ½-inch-
thick wooden dowel at a hardware or crafts store and
cut it into 10-inch lengths. Make this pasta with a friend,
spouse, or older child, as it does take time—providing an
opportunity for busy hands and leisurely conversations.
Now that's a gift, too.

Prep Time and Rest Time for Dough: 50 minutes | Rolling Time for Pasta: 2
hours | Makes a generous 2 pounds garganelli, portioned into three (4-serving)
packages

---

1 Place half of the flour in the bowl of a stand mixer fitted with
   the paddle attachment. Add the eggs and begin mixing on low
   speed until the ingredients come together. Add the remaining
   flour in 2 batches, mixing on low speed after each addition.
   (The mixer will be working hard and might strain a little; if so,
   turn the mixer off, pull the dough down from the blades, and
   begin to mix again.)

2 Once the dough comes together, turn the mixer off and switch to the dough hook. Knead the dough for 12 minutes, stopping the mixer from time to time if the dough crawls up the dough hook. Remove the dough and wrap it tightly in plastic wrap. Set aside at room temperature for 30 minutes. This allows the gluten to relax. (The pasta dough can be wrapped tightly in plastic wrap and refrigerated for up to 3 days or frozen for up to 3 weeks. Bring the dough to room temperature before rolling and cutting.)

3 To make the garganelli, use a bench knife to cut a lemon-size piece of dough. Tightly rewrap the remaining dough as you work with each portion. Position the rollers on a pasta machine at the widest setting, and pass the dough through the rollers 6 or 7 times, folding the dough in half lengthwise and pressing it together before each pass. Lightly dust the dough with flour, only if needed. Reset the rollers to the next narrower setting and pass the dough through the rollers 2 times, without folding over the dough. Continue to reset the rollers, passing the dough through each setting 2 times. The next-to-last setting is the final setting for the desired thickness of dough. Before passing the dough through this setting, dust the dough lightly with flour, as it will be a bit tacky. As the dough passes through the rollers, be careful to keep it stretched out and don't let it overlap in folded layers, as it will stick together.

4 Lightly dust a work surface with flour. Carefully lay out the dough. Using a fluted pastry cutter, trim the edges of the dough into a long rectangle. Measure and cut the dough into 2-inch squares. The ends will be oddly shaped, so trim them as best you can, and use them because the pasta shape is rustic and charming. Cover the cut sheet of dough with lightly dampened paper towels. Orient the sushi mat so the bamboo strips run parallel to the edge of the counter. Working with 2 squares of dough at a time, position the squares in a diamond shape and about a finger-width apart on the end of the mat closest to the edge of the counter. Position the wooden dowel parallel to the edge of the counter, and lay it across the center of the diamonds. Lift the pointed end of each diamond closest to you, and roll it over the dowel. Roll the dowel away from you, wrapping the dough around the dowel. Gently press the dough against the bamboo mat as you roll, imprinting ridges into the dough. Continue to roll the dough to the opposite end of the mat to fully imprint the dough with ridges. Transfer the rolled pasta to a clean, dry towel. Continue until all the squares have been rolled.

5 Repeat steps 3 and 4 until all the dough has been used.

6 Let the garganelli dry at room temperature, rolling the pasta on the towel from time to time to expose all the surfaces to the air. Dry the pasta until all the moisture is gone and the pasta feels completely dry and hard, about 24 hours.

STORING: *Store in a tightly covered tin or glass container. (Do not store in plastic bags, as there is no breathability and the dried pasta can get moldy.) The pasta will keep for 1 month when kept in a cool, dry place.*

GIFT CARD: This Homemade Garganelli was made on [give date]. Keep in a cool, dry place until ready to use. To cook the garganelli, bring a large pot of water to a boil, add salt, and then add the pasta. Stir and cook the pasta until al dente (cooked through, but still slightly chewy, 8 to 10 minutes. Taste for doneness. Drain the pasta in a colander, but do not rinse. Add the pasta to your favorite marinara or Bolognese sauce and toss gently to combine and coat the pasta. Divide the pasta among warmed bowls, shower with freshly grated Parmesan, and serve immediately. Serves 4.

GIFT-GIVING TIPS: Portion the garganelli into 3 cellophane bags and tie them with raffia or ribbon. Attach a gift card. To turn this into a gift basket, consider including a bottle of Italian extra-virgin olive oil and a hunk of Parmigiano-Reggiano cheese. To make the gift a bit more elaborate, see page 170 for a gift kit idea.

SEVEN-MONTH VANILLA EXTRACT

INGREDIENTS

9 whole vanilla beans

1 tablespoon dark rum

1 (750-milliliter) bottle premium vodka

IMPLEMENTS

Three (7- to 8-Ounce) Glass Bottles with a Screw Top or Hinge Cap, Paring Knife, Cutting Board, Measuring Spoon, Narrow-Neck Funnel

Anyone who loves to bake will treasure this present, and you don't even have to bake to make these gifts! There's nothing to it: Select attractive glass bottles; buy plump vanilla beans, rum, and vodka; slit the beans and fit them into the bottles; pour the liquor over the top; and seal. Either make the vanilla and store it for months or give it freshly made and let the recipient watch it turn from light amber to a deep, luscious brown. It's an especially treasured gift because it keeps on giving—just replenish the amount in the bottle by adding vodka to re-cover the beans.

Prep Time: 20 minutes | Infusing Time: 7 months | Makes three (7- to 8-ounce) bottles of vanilla extract

1 Wash the bottles, including the lids, in hot, soapy water and dry thoroughly. Alternatively, run the bottles through the regular cycle of your dishwasher; wash the lids by hand.

2 Using a sharp paring knife, carefully slit the vanilla beans lengthwise to expose the seeds, without cutting the bean in half. Fit 3 vanilla beans into each bottle.

3 Using a narrow-neck funnel, pour 1 teaspoon of rum into each bottle. Add enough vodka to cover the beans completely, leaving ½ inch headspace. Wipe the rims, secure the lids, and label.

RECIPE CARD: CREATE A CARD TO PACKAGE WITH GIFT

CRÈME BRÛLÉE

Preheat the oven to 300°F. Set six (6-ounce) ramekins in a roasting pan. Bring 3 cups heavy cream to a boil. Set aside. Whisk together 6 large egg yolks, ¾ cup sugar, 2 t. vanilla extract, and ¾ t. salt. Slowly add the cream and whisk until smooth. Strain the mixture into a 4-cup glass measuring cup or bowl. Fill the ramekins. Place in the oven, and pour hot water into the roasting pan to come halfway up the sides. Bake until the centers are set, 30 to 35 minutes. Lift from the water and cool on a wire rack. Cover and refrigerate. Sprinkle 1 T. of sugar evenly over each custard. Broil until the sugar bubbles and turns caramel color. Serve immediately. Serves 6.

STORING: *Store the bottles in a cool, dark place, gently shaking the bottles once a week. The vanilla is ready to use 7 months from the date it was made.*

GIFT CARD: This homemade Seven-Month Vanilla Extract was bottled on [give date] and can be enjoyed for up to 7 years—just replenish the used portion by adding vodka to cover the beans. Leave set in a cool, dark place for 7 months, shaking the bottle once a week.

GIFT-GIVING TIPS: Tie each bottle with raffia or ribbon and attach a gift card. To turn this into a gift basket, add the recipe that follows for crème brûlée, a half-dozen fresh eggs from the farmers' market, some organic heavy cream, and, if desired, 6 traditional white porcelain crème brûlée dishes. You could even add a chef's torch!

CHAPTER 12

MAKE-A-*gift* KITS

How do we take these delectable gifts and package them cleverly to create more elaborate presents? This chapter is an exciting grab bag of unique and crafty ways to package up your edible offerings into grander presents for those occasions when a showier gift is called for. Let your creativity flow as you mix and match to make a gift kit, wrapping and delivering a present that speaks from the heart and elicits an enthusiastic smile.

S'MORES KIT

To create a S'Mores Kit, there are two delectable recipes in the book to combine for gift giving—the Toasted Coconut Marshmallows and the Cinnamon-Coated Graham Crackers. How fun to combine these, package them in an artful and clever way, and deliver this sweet treat as a favorite cookout dessert, especially when children are involved. Who doesn't have fond memories of sitting around a campfire roasting marshmallows carefully poked onto thin, stripped tree branches, turning just enough to caramelize the sugar and make them puffy and hot?

As a summertime gift when invited to a backyard barbecue, wrap and package Toasted Coconut Marshmallows along with Cinnamon-Coated Graham Crackers and bars of chocolate in a fanciful box ready for assembly as a nostalgic dessert. As a clever and thoughtful addition, include grill skewers for roasting the marshmallows, this way everything is ready for dessert-time fun. Though the tradition when making s'mores is to use not-very-fancy milk chocolate bars, consider how much more fun it would be to buy deliciously decadent artisanal chocolate and make dark chocolate s'mores.

Consider giving a S'Mores Kit as a thank you gift when spending a weekend at a friend's mountain cabin. After all, wintertime ski vacations are another opportunity for child-like fun when warming frosty toes around a roaring fire could also mean toasting marshmallows and having a well-deserved après-ski treat. Be sure to bring along plenty of extras to last the whole weekend through!

A weekend getaway with gal pals, especially childhood friends, would be another opportunity to share a homemade gift and make a S'Mores Kit. Just think of all the tales from camp, middle school memories, and high school capers that could be remembered and laughed about while roasting marshmallows and licking fingers from melting chocolate, all the while munching on crispy delicious graham crackers.

CHEESE KIT

To create a Cheese Kit, there are several recipes in *Gifts Cooks Love* that would be ideal to package and expand into a larger gift. The Green Tomato Chutney, the Aleppo Pepper–Peach Chutney, the Panforte, the Rustic Rosemary-Parmesan Crackers, and the Chipotle Chile Candied Pecans all make a cheese course or cheese appetizer more spectacular. The chutney can be poured over cream cheese and served with crackers. Consider packaging one or two of these food gifts in a creative way and expanding your gift to include accessories for the cheese lovers in your life.

As a hostess or thank-you gift, one of these food gifts alone might be enough, but a cheese knife, slicer, or plane tied with the bow would look great. Consider including porcelain cheese markers, cheese paper, or even a set of cheese spreaders.

For the cheese geeks on your gift list, buy a set of cheese picks. These delightful animal-shaped porcelain markers follow the French tradition of designating cheese by milk type—cow, sheep, and goat. With the picks and a selection of cheeses, including a wedge of the Panforte would complete the offering of an amazing cheese course.

For those who love to throw parties, a fun wedding, birthday, or housewarming gift could include the Green Tomato Chutney or Aleppo Pepper–Peach Chutney along with a petite cheese knife set and cheese board—either marble, Italian ceramic, or bamboo. Match the cheese platter with a coordinating condiment bowl, and include a hunk of aged Gouda to complete the gift.

As a ready-to-eat gift, arrange the Rustic Rosemary-Parmesan Crackers on a long white ceramic cheese platter along with artisan cheeses, such as a log of creamy goat cheese and a wedge of farmstead cheddar. Wrap the entire platter with clear cellophane and tie it in a rustic style with raffia; or for a holiday party, tie the gift with a big red or gold bow and attach a cheese-themed ornament.

Enjoy!

BREAKFAST KIT

RECITES

Who doesn't want to wake up to a homemade food gift? Imagine brightening someone's morning with yummy, ready-to-eat breakfast or brunch fare. There is a bounty of recipes in *Gifts Cooks Love* that would be ideal to package and expand into a larger gift: the Meyer Lemon Curd; the Orange-Cardamom Marmalade; the Boysenberry and Lemon Verbena Jam; the Salmon Gravlax; Benny's Bacon; the Mini Apricot and Crystallized Ginger Quick Breads; the Jalapeño and Cheddar Skillet Cornbread with Honey Butter; the Coconut Granola Crunch; and the Mexican Drinking Chocolate.

As a thank-you gift, Benny's Bacon, wrapped in butcher paper and tied with butcher's twine and accompanied by brown eggs from the farmers' market, could be packaged in a large cast-iron skillet and wrapped with a colorful kitchen towel.

Heading to a friend's home for the weekend? Bring a teatime offering of Meyer Lemon Curd or Orange-Cardamom Marmalade packaged with scones or even a scone mix, a porcelain teapot, and a selection of herbal teas. Consider a breakfast basket overflowing with Coconut Granola Crunch, a set of bistro-style breakfast bowls, containers of yogurt, and fresh fruit. Boysenberry and Lemon Verbena Jam and a crusty loaf of artisan bread ready for toasting would certainly be another breakfast favorite.

Mini Apricot and Crystallized Ginger Quick Breads, a favorite to make at holiday time, would be a welcome hostess gift packaged in a rustic, earthenware bread basket lined with a tea towel and tied with a coordinating bow. Another holiday favorite is to give the Mexican Drinking Chocolate along with a set of festive red cappuccino cups. Any time of year, the Jalapeño and Cheddar Skillet Cornbread with Honey Butter, baked and delivered in a cast-iron skillet, would also delight a host.

For the late sleepers in your life, for whom breakfast looks more like brunch, let them wake up to a Scandinavian or Jewish meal of Salmon Gravlax, artisan cream cheese, and either bagels or rye flatbreads. Package it all in a rustic bread basket; or you could arrange the salmon on a wooden board and include a decorative slicing knife and spreader, wrapping the gift in cellophane with the spreader tied into the bow.

RECIPES

To create a Pasta Kit, there are three recipes in *Gifts Cooks Love* that would be perfect to package and expand into a larger gift: the Dried Porcini Mushrooms, the Arrabbiata Sauce, and the Homemade Garganelli.

As a gift for the cooking enthusiast, package the Homemade Garganelli with a pasta maker, a bag of the tipo "OO" flour, and the recipe for making garganelli. You could even include a bamboo sushi mat and precut dowels. Arrange it in a basket lined with a linen towel, wrap it with a large sheet of clear cellophane, and tie it with a big raffia bow.

For a wedding, birthday, or housewarming gift, give one of the suggested food gifts set inside a pasta pot, large pasta serving bowl, or colander. Include a pasta server or cheese grater, if desired. You could certainly include a hunk of Parmigiano-Reggiano cheese or a bottle of olive oil, depending on how elaborate you want the gift to be.

As a hostess or thank-you gift, include a simple pasta tool or gadget along with the food gift. For instance, as you tie ribbon around the jar of Arrabbiata Sauce, it would look great to secure a pasta server, pair of tongs, or handheld cheese grater within the knot of the bow. Even a linen towel imprinted with an Italian motif could be the wrapping for any one of these food gifts.

RETRO POPCORN KIT

RECIPES

So many friends and families are bringing movie night back home; why not give a gift that delivers the big screen experience and the tubs of buttery popped popcorn, too? *Gifts Cooks Love* has recipes that are rated "G" for general audience munching.

To create a retro popcorn kit, package the Home-Churned Lemon-Herb Butter on page 149 along with a stovetop, hand-cranked aluminum popper and a jar of White Cat Corn, the premium gourmet popcorn in the United States. Another idea is to include a nostalgic collection of old-fashioned paper popcorn boxes, which turns movie night into an exciting evening at the theater.

A perfect gift for modern movie buffs—namely, those who only know microwave popcorn—is the innovative microwave popper that requires no cooking oil and has a special lid that drips butter onto the fresh corn as it pops. Turn the popcorn out into a bowl and shake on the aromatic Bollywood Coconut Curry Popcorn Seasoning on page 151.

Simple enough for a hostess or thank-you gift would be the Home-Churned Lemon-Herb Butter or the Bollywood Coconut Curry Popcorn Seasoning, packaged along with a jar of premium gourmet popcorn and set inside a porcelain popcorn bowl reminiscent of the old-fashioned theater popcorn boxes.

GRILL KIT

To create a Grill Kit, there are several recipes in *Gifts Cooks Love* that would be ideal to package and expand into a larger gift: the Aleppo Pepper–Peach Chutney is divine with grilled chicken; the Smoky Tomato Ketchup is fun for a summertime burger fest; the Backyard BBQ Rub is the go-to dry rub for grilling; the Côtes du Rhône–Rhubarb Compote is perfect with grilled pork.

As a gift for the grilling enthusiast, package the Backyard BBQ Rub, along with the recipe, inside a stainless-steel grill basket and include grill tools or even grill skewers. Since this rub is so versatile and terrific on grilled corn on the cob, you could package it with a corn grilling cage, corn holders, and glass corn dishes. Another idea is to include the rub with grilling planks, as it is fabulous on grilled salmon. Adding a wide, long stainless-steel spatula will make it easy for the griller to lift the planks off the grill. Wrap it all with a large sheet of clear cellophane and tie it with a big, summery, red-and-white checked bow.

For those on your gift list who love throwing summer cookouts, a fun wedding, birthday, or housewarming gift could include the Smoky Tomato Ketchup along with a double burger press, burger grilling basket, spatula, and set of burger baskets with red-checked paper liners.

The Aleppo Pepper–Peach Chutney, a perfect accompaniment to grilled chicken, could be matched with a vertical roaster for the grill master. The tipsy beer can that so cleverly supports a whole chicken for grill-roasting has been replaced with a stable and sturdy grill accessory.

As a hostess or thank-you gift, the food gift alone might be enough, but a grill tool or gadget tied with the bow would look great. Consider a set of barbecue skewers, long grill mitts, or even a snazzy grill apron.

ACKNOWLEDGMENTS

When we think of what our customers love to do best, one activity rises to the top—giving their loved ones gifts from their own kitchen.

There is no one that could have communicated that message more adeptly than Diane Morgan. A consummate professional, Diane has it all: a can-do attitude, creativity, enthusiasm, and an ability to master any task presented to her with panache. "No problem" is her mantra. Sur La Table was thrilled to have Diane lead the charge on *Gifts Cooks Love,* and was assisted in the synergy created in this book by the photographic magic of Sara Remington and her assistant Stacy Ventura, the food styling wizardry of Kim Kissling and her assistant Tina Stamos, and the awe-inspiring prop styling of Kerrie Walsh and her assistant Lori Ehlers. Jenny Barry's personal love for making beautiful food gifts, clever packaging tricks, and decorations drove the vision and tied the bow on this beautiful gift to everyone who loves to give the gift of food.

Thanks to Mike and Kathy Tierney for sharing their home and providing generous hospitality for the photo shoot; to the staff of the Brewery Blocks store for being there when Diane needed them; to Deb Pankrat and Audrey Borreani at the Berkeley store for amazing customer service; to Kate Dering, Cindy Payne, Linda Nangle, Claudia Saber, Tony Dellino, Sue Pippy, and Alycia Johnson for product assistance; to Robb Ginter and the creative department at Sur La Table for their tireless efforts to make this book special; to Razonia McClellan, Tammie Barker, and Amy Worley for making sure no stone is left unturned; and to Morgan McQuade, Dave Bauer, and Mark Beard for making sure the merchandise was in the right place at the right time. To the folks at Andrews McMeel, especially Kirsty Melville and Jean Lucas—thank you for supporting our ideas and for always being there when we need you. And thank you to our agent, Janis Donnaud, our anchor in the storm.

But most important, we thank our customers, who continually provide us inspiration to create gifts cooks love.

—Sur La Table

In the spirit of gift giving, when family, friends, and colleagues are remembered and acknowledged for making life special and every day a blessing, I have an important list of people deserving a huge thank-you gift, all wrapped up in festive paper and tied with a huge bow.

To Doralece Dullaghan, director of Strategic Partnerships at Sur La Table, for all your expert guidance, time, and support over the years. You have given me opportunities to teach in every Sur La Table cooking school across the country, and now the gift of asking me to write this book. I am deeply grateful for our professional relationship and long friendship.

To the entire team at Sur La Table, who have all been so supportive, creative, and enthusiastic about this book, I offer my heartfelt thanks.

To Kirsty Melville, Jean Lucas, and everyone else at Andrews McMeel Publishing, who have attentively supported this book and kept it on track—your talents and keen sense of detail have made this writing and editing process a success.

To Sara Remington, Jennifer Barry, Kim Kissling, and Kerrie Walsh, your creativity, sense of style, and perfectionism are the reasons this book is so beautifully conceived and lusciously photographed. It has been a delight working with all of you.

To Lisa Ekus, my agent, for all your insights, support, and amazing advice—you are a treasure in my life.

To Andrea Slonecker, my dedicated and trusted assistant—you have made developing and testing recipes both a pleasure and a creative time. I enjoy your youthful spirit and infectious laugh—and there have been plenty of days in the kitchen when we needed that!

To Harriet and Peter Watson, for your dear friendship and spirit. You brighten my day—every day. Many thanks to my friends and family for their generosity and love: Richard and Barb LevKoy; Larry LevKoy; Irene LevKoy; Roxane, Austin, Joey, and Tommy Huang; Steve and Marci Taylor; Margie Miller; Priscilla and John Longfield; Cheryl Russell; Josie Jimenez; Karen Fong; Summer Jameson; Sherry Gable; Elissa Altman; Domenica Marchetti; Tori Ritchie; Joyce Goldstein; Braiden Rex-Johnson; Bill and Adair Lara; Jolene George; Lisa Hill; and Laura Werlin.

Finally, my beloved thanks to the most treasured gifts of my lifetime: my husband, Greg, and my children, Eric and Molly.

—Diane Morgan

METRIC CONVERSIONS
& EQUIVALENTS

METRIC CONVERSION FORMULAS

TO CONVERT	MULTIPLY
Ounces to grams	Ounces by 28.35
Pounds to kilograms	Pounds by 0.454
Teaspoons to milliliters	Teaspoons by 4.93
Tablespoons to milliliters	Tablespoons by 14.79
Fluid ounces to milliliters	Fluid ounces by 29.57
Cups to milliliters	Cups by 236.59
Cups to liters	Cups by 0.236
Pints to liters	Pints by 0.473
Quarts to liters	Quarts by 0.946
Gallons to liters	Gallons by 3.785
Inches to centimeters	Inches by 2.54

COMMON INGREDIENTS AND THEIR APPROXIMATE EQUIVALENTS

1 cup uncooked white rice = 185 grams

1 cup all-purpose flour = 140 grams

1 stick butter (4 ounces • ½ cup • 8 tablespoons) = 110 grams

1 cup butter (8 ounces • 2 sticks • 16 tablespoons) = 220 grams

1 cup brown sugar, firmly packed = 225 grams

1 cup granulated sugar = 200 grams

OVEN TEMPERATURES

To convert Fahrenheit to Celsius, subtract 32 from Fahrenheit, multiply the result by 5, then divide by 9.

DESCRIPTION	FAHRENHEIT	CELSIUS	BRITISH GAS MARK
Very cool	200°	95°	0
Very cool	225°	110°	¼
Very cool	250°	120°	½
Cool	275°	135°	1
Cool	300°	150°	2
Warm	325°	165°	3
Moderate	350°	175°	4
Moderately hot	375°	190°	5
Fairly hot	400°	200°	6
Hot	425°	220°	7
Very hot	450°	230°	8
Very hot	475°	245°	9

APPROXIMATE METRIC EQUIVALENTS

VOLUME

¼ teaspoon	1 milliliter
½ teaspoon	2.5 milliliters
¾ teaspoon	4 milliliters
1 teaspoon	5 milliliters
1¼ teaspoons	6 milliliters
1½ teaspoons	7.5 milliliters
1¾ teaspoons	8.5 milliliters
2 teaspoons	10 milliliters
1 tablespoon (½ fluid ounce)	15 milliliters
2 tablespoons (1 fluid ounce)	30 milliliters
¼ cup	60 milliliters
⅓ cup	80 milliliters
½ cup (4 fluid ounces)	120 milliliters
⅔ cup	160 milliliters
¾ cup	180 milliliters
1 cup (8 fluid ounces)	240 milliliters
1¼ cups	300 milliliters
1½ cups (12 fluid ounces)	360 milliliters
1⅔ cups	400 milliliters
2 cups (1 pint)	460 milliliters
3 cups	700 milliliters
4 cups (1 quart)	0.95 liter
1 quart plus ¼ cup	1 liter
4 quarts (1 gallon)	3.8 liters

WEIGHT

¼ ounce	7 grams
½ ounce	14 grams
¾ ounce	21 grams
1 ounce	28 grams
1¼ ounces	35 grams
1½ ounces	42.5 grams
1⅔ ounces	45 grams
2 ounces	57 grams
3 ounces	85 grams
4 ounces (¼ pound)	113 grams
5 ounces	142 grams
6 ounces	170 grams
7 ounces	198 grams
8 ounces (½ pound)	227 grams
16 ounces (1 pound)	454 grams
35.25 ounces (2.2 pounds)	1 kilogram

LENGTH

⅛ inch	3 millimeters
¼ inch	6 millimeters
½ inch	1¼ centimeters
1 inch	2½ centimeters
2 inches	5 centimeters
2½ inches	6 centimeters
4 inches	10 centimeters
5 inches	13 centimeters
6 inches	15¼ centimeters
12 inches (1 foot)	30 centimeters

Information compiled from a variety of sources, including *Recipes into Type* by Joan Whitman and Dolores Simon (Newton, MA: Biscuit Books, 2000); *The New Food Lover's Companion* by Sharon Tyler Herbst (Hauppauge, NY: Barron's, 1995); and *Rosemary Brown's Big Kitchen Instruction Book* (Kansas City, MO: Andrews McMeel, 1998).

INDEX